PRACTICAL GUIDE TO
SYNTACTIC ANALYSIS, 2nd edition

PRACTICAL GUIDE TO
SYNTACTIC ANALYSIS, 2nd edition

Georgia M. Green and Jerry L. Morgan

CSLI PUBLICATIONS Center for the Study of
Language and Information
Stanford, California

To our children,
who have reinforced our beliefs about
the powers of explanation.

Copyright © 2001
CSLI Publications
Center for the Study of Language and Information
Leland Stanford Junior University
Printed in the United States
05 04 03 02 01   5 4 3 2 1

Library of Congress Cataloging-in-Publication Data

Green, Georgia M.
Practical guide to syntactic analysis /
Georgia M. Green and Jerry L. Morgan.– 2nd ed.
p.   cm. — (CSLI lecture notes ; no. 135)
Includes bibliographical references and index.

ISBN 1-57586-348-0 (paper : alk. paper)
ISBN 1-57586-349-9 (cloth : alk. paper)

1. Grammar, Comparative and general–Syntax.
I. Morgan, Jerry L.
II. Title. III. Series.
P291.G694   2002
415—dc21   2001058107
CIP

∞ The acid-free paper used in this book meets the minimum requirements of the American National Standard for Information Sciences—Permanence of Paper for Printed Library Materials, ANSI Z39.48-1984.

CSLI was founded early in 1983 by researchers from Stanford University, SRI International, and Xerox PARC to further research and development of integrated theories of language, information, and computation. CSLI headquarters and CSLI Publications are located on the campus of Stanford University.

CSLI Publications reports new developments in the study of language, information, and computation. In addition to lecture notes, our publications include monographs, working papers, revised dissertations, and conference proceedings. Our aim is to make new results, ideas, and approaches available as quickly as possible. Please visit our web site at
http://cslipublications.stanford.edu/
for comments on this and other titles, as well as for changes and corrections by the author and publisher.

CONTENTS

PREFACE TO THE SECOND EDITION

This second edition clarifies the prose in a few passages that were less than clear, and updates some of the theory discussion. More noticeably, it includes an appendix containing an annotated list of syntactic phenomena common in languages across the world, with examples from English. The descriptions there have been framed to be as theory-neutral as possible, so that their utility may outlast the inevitable shifts in syntactic theory. Students who seek theory-specific analyses of particular phenomena are encouraged to take advantage of class discussions. The new appendix also includes, for the first time, information about pragmatic correlates of a number of syntactic constructions.

The publication of the appended reference guide is dedicated to all of our skeptical colleagues who said it couldn't be done: description of syntactic phenomena with virtually no procedural metaphors.

Acknowledgments

Grateful thanks to our colleagues Abbas Benmamoun and James Yoon for comments on previous versions.
Georgia M. Green
Jerry L. Morgan
Urbana, 2001

PREFACE

This book is intended as a resource for students of syntax at all levels, supplementary to their textbooks and class discussions. It takes for granted that the student has a basic understanding of why one might want to describe natural language within the general framework of generative grammar. It offers:

1. A thorough discussion (Chapter 1) of the fundamental assumptions of the study of syntax, at a level of detail which facilitates seeing the forest as well as the trees.

2. Guidance in doing and presenting syntactic analysis (Chapters 2-4). The discussion of argumentation and presentation is applicable not just to syntax, but to phonology, pragmatics, and semantics as well, and probably much more generally. This will still be useful long after analyses published this year are out of date.

3. A brief account of the so-called Standard Theory (Chapter 5), and how the major current frameworks for syntactic description have evolved to differ from it (Chapters 6-7). For more detail on their motivation and the sorts of accounts and analyses they offer, the reader is referred to the original works describing these theories.

This book does not provide a glossary of technical terms in syntax. Such a glossary would no doubt be desirable in a guide of this sort. Unfortunately, the technical terms in contemporary syntactic theory tend to be very unstable and short-lived; how linguist X defines a term in a certain paper may differ from the way linguist Y uses it in a different paper. As a consequence, unless a glossary recapitulated the history of terms as well as the range of meanings of terms, it would be likely to generate more confusion than enlightenment. We urge readers to use their wits to track down what particular linguists mean by the terms they use, and to keep in mind that it isn't always possible to tell exactly what a term is being used to refer to–sometimes writers fail to say exactly what they mean by some term that figures crucially in their analysis. It is not an acceptable practice, but it sometimes happens anyway.

The sections may be usefully consulted in any order.

Although this book contains discussion of the evolution of various descriptive devices, intended to enable the reader to form a context for understanding both current and older issues in the linguistic literature, it does not describe the motivations for classical transformational grammar, the mathematical foundations of it, or the history of generative grammar. It is certainly not intended to be a comprehensive history of syntactic thought, even of syntactic thought of the last 20 years.[1]

Some of the topics discussed (e.g., cyclic rule application, global rules) may seem at first out of date. We feel it is important to include them insofar as they provide a means for understanding the context in which subsequent theoretical proposals were made, and for appreciating their antecedents. The increasing frequency with which previously abandoned approaches to a variety of problems have been unwittingly resurrected in recent years speaks volumes about why the older literature needs to be kept accessible.

Acknowledgments

We are grateful to Linda May, whose LAT$_E$X wizardry helped make this Guide much more visually attractive than its typescript predecessors, and to generations of students who used five different preliminary versions of this book.

This work was supported in part by the Beckman Institute for Advanced Science and Technology at the University of Illinois at Urbana-Champaign.

Georgia M. Green
Jerry L. Morgan
Urbana, 1996

---

[1]For a detailed analysis of the syntactic constructions of English, the reader is referred to McCawley (1988). Newmeyer (1986), Harris (1993), and Huck & Goldsmith (1995) provide a variety of colorful accounts of the development of syntactic theory up to about 1985; Sells (1985) provides detailed descriptions of three approaches current at that time.

NOTATIONAL CONVENTIONS USED IN THIS BOOK

Italics mark cited expressions.

Single quotes (' ') enclose meanings of forms.

Double quotes (" ") enclose quoted expressions.

Bold face marks important expressions whose meaning is explained or implied in the text.

An asterisk (*) marks an expression being claimed to be ungrammatical.

1 WHAT A GRAMMAR IS, AND ISN'T

Why is linguistic theory so widely misunderstood that in a 1989 collection of essays called *Reflections on Chomsky* (George 1989), a chapter could be titled "How not to become confused about linguistics"? Generative linguistic theory as it has grown out of the work of Noam Chomsky (1955, 1957, 1965, 1975, 1981, 1986a) has profound implications not only for linguistics, but also, insofar as it has important things to say about the human mind and human nature, for other domains of inquiry, including psychology and philosophy. So it is no surprise that it has provoked impassioned reactions, both pro and con, not only in linguistics but in several neighboring fields. But the critiques are often wide of the mark, since they are based on a thorough misunderstanding of the foundations of generative theory (see George 1989). These same misunderstandings are often found among beginning students of linguistics.

It may be that part of the problem is the difficult writing style of Chomsky and some of his followers. But we suspect that a greater part of the blame is due to critics' failure to consider carefully the whole picture of the generative approach, in particular the view of mind that it is based on. And we have no doubt that many misconceptions are due to an unfortunate choice of metaphorical terminology on the part of linguists who use generative theory. The purpose of this chapter is to bring these problems into the light, in order to reduce the likelihood that the student will be distracted by these misconceptions.

We begin by discussing the goals of linguistic theory, and how the concept of a grammar fits into the framework of those goals. We then discuss some common metaphors that may mislead the unwary student, and some criticisms of generative grammar that have a certain superficial appeal, but turn out to be misguided when they are examined closely.

1

1.1 Goals of Linguistic Theory

To properly understand generative grammar, and what counts as valid criticism of work in that framework, it is essential to understand the theoretical goals that are being pursued. Chomsky's position on the goals of linguistic theory is by far the dominant one in the field. The most important point of his position is this: the goals of linguistic theory are psychological. Language is a mental phenomenon, to be studied as such, and theories of language are to be considered as psychological theories. So the object of study is the human mind, and it is the nature of the human mind as reflected in the acquisition and use of language that provides the central questions of the field. This approach to the scientific study of language is by now so common-place that it is hard to imagine things being otherwise. But Chomsky's immediate predecessors in American linguistics had a quite different position, one in which language was (at least in theory) studied as a kind of natural object, and questions of mind were to be avoided at all costs. Even now there are theories with quite different goals. For some varieties of Montague grammar (Montague 1970, 1973; Dowty, Wall, and Peters 1981), for example, questions of psychology are largely irrelevant. Katz (1981) proposes a Platonic approach to the study of language, which rejects Chomsky's psychological goals. But most syntacticians, at least if pressed, would admit to being Chomskyan in their theoretical goals, though perhaps differing with Chomsky (and each other) on other points.

For such an approach to linguistics, it is not language (whatever is meant by that slippery term) but **knowledge of language** that is the central phenomenon to be studied and explained. The term generally used to refer to that knowledge is **grammar**. But to fully appreciate the details of the Chomskyan program, it is necessary always to keep in mind Chomsky's goals and assumptions about the mind, including especially these:

(1) THE MIND IS INNATELY STRUCTURED. For Chomsky, the mind is not a blank slate, but a highly structured organ whose structure is determined in large part by genetically governed (though poorly understood) properties of the brain. This position differs sharply from the widely held position that the brain and mind have little innate structure, but are shaped almost entirely by experience. More specifically, it is Chomsky's view that:

(2) THE MIND IS MODULAR. According to this Modularity Hypothesis, the human mind does not consist of a single all-purpose structure, but has sub-parts that are specialized in function for particular cognitive and perceptual domains. This structure is presumed to reflect (perhaps indirectly) physical properties of the brain. It is an open question—to be settled by scientific

means, not a priori philosophical ones—whether the modularity hypothesis is correct, and if it is correct, what substructures the mind contains. The modularity position does not imply (this is an important point) complete modular autonomy in operation: since most cognitive tasks humans face are not purely of one kind or another, most things we do presumably involve the interaction of several faculties. The existence of such interaction is not in itself a threat to the modularity hypothesis. Sadock (1983) elaborates insightfully on this point.

(3) THERE IS A DISTINCT MODULE FOR LANGUAGE. Among the faculties hypothesized to make up the mind, Chomsky argues, is one specific to language. There are two important points to keep in mind here. First, the modularity hypothesis does not depend on the existence of a language faculty; the mind could be modular without there being a language faculty, though of course if there is a language faculty the mind is *ipso facto* modular. Second, it should be clear that something like Chomsky's position has always been implicit in the study of language (though perhaps not consciously in the minds of the investigators) in that grammarians have generally approached language as something that can reasonably be isolated for study apart from other human activities or artifacts. If what we call language is really inherently inseparable from other mental abilities, then the study of language makes no more sense as a coherent science than the study of knowledge of things made in Michigan. Chomsky's position on the modularity of language provides a coherent rationale for this traditional isolation of language for study.

(4) LANGUAGE ACQUISITION IS THE CENTRAL PUZZLE FOR LINGUISTIC THEORY. Just what functions the hypothesized language faculty has is an open question; for Chomsky, the primary purpose of the language faculty is for learning language. It might serve this function either by being a learning mechanism itself, or by somehow interacting with a learning mechanism to determine the course of language learning. For Chomsky, the language faculty and its function are the central concern of linguistic theory, and understandably so. To the linguist who has looked in depth at the awesome complexity of the grammar of any language, it seems a miracle that a small child could master such a system in such a short time. Explaining this apparent miracle is the problem of **explanatory adequacy**, which is for Chomsky the central goal of linguistic theory. The explanation is to be given by investigating the language faculty, to determine its structure and contents, and how it makes it possible for a child to learn a human language. Chomsky's position is that the language faculty is structured in such a way that the child, when faced with the **primary data** of language presented by the senses, has a very limited set of options available for constructing a grammar consistent with those primary data. So

the child's choices in the language learning task are narrowly constrained by physical properties of the brain, which are in turn determined by the child's genes. (These brain structures are not fully formed at birth, but it is genetically predetermined that they will develop eventually if the physical development of the child follows its normal course, just as with many other genetically determined properties.)

Given this picture of things, it follows that two children faced with roughly similar linguistic experience are bound to come up with similar grammars, insofar as their language faculties are similar. And insofar as the language faculty is a reflection of genetically determined properties of the brain, two normal children should have roughly similar language faculties, if we assume no more genetic variation there than in other genetically determined properties.

This general position is known as the Innateness Hypothesis. Its essence is that every human is genetically endowed with the potential to develop certain brain structures which influence the course and outcome of language acquisition, by in effect setting limits on what kind of grammar a child can construct when faced with the data of linguistic experience. A theory that provides an account of this innate structure, and thus an explanation of how language can be learned, achieves the Chomskyan goal of explanatory adequacy. And it is the Innateness Hypothesis that makes the study of **universal grammar** relevant for linguistic theory. Given that the inherited biology of the brain strongly guides language acquisition in certain directions, we should expect to find consequences of such biological facts in terms of properties all languages share, or strongly tend to share. And certain properties should be rare or nonexistent because the inherited language faculty makes it very difficult or impossible for a human to learn a language with those properties. So detailed analysis and comparison of the grammars of a significant variety of languages is a crucial source of potential data on the structure of the language faculty.

That is not to say, though, that all universal properties are of equal importance for this view of language. There may well be properties all languages share that have no relevance to the goal of explanatory adequacy (that is, the goal of discovering the workings of the innate language faculty). For example, it is very likely that every language has a word meaning what the English word *mother* means. This fact is most likely to be explained in terms of human needs: mothers are biologically and psychologically very important in all human cultures, and languages tend to have words for referring to things that are important to language users. Although this putative universal tells us something profound about human nature, it tells us nothing about the language faculty, so it is not a significant fact in the approach to universal grammar that pursues the goal of explanatory adequacy.

(5) SYNTAX IS FORMAL. Another crucial aspect of Chomsky's view is that language is represented in the mind, and to be studied by the linguist, as a formal system. There is a potential source of confusion here in the use of the term *formal*. This is a position on the NATURE of LANGUAGE, and it is important not to confuse it with the methodological principle that THEORIES of language should be framed in some interpreted formal system. The latter sense of the expression *formal syntax* has to do with what counts as a useful theory, and is entirely independent of the nature of language. In principle, one could have a fully formalized theory of language that described language in terms of communicative function (there is no such theory at present, but that is beside the point—there could be such a theory). The essence of the former sense of *formal syntax* (sometimes referred to as *the autonomy of syntax*) is that principles of syntax have to do just with matters of linguistic form, and are independent (in the mind, hence also in the correct theory) of matters of meaning or communicative function. This is not a methodological point, it is a position (possibly incorrect) on the facts. Obviously the primary function of language is for communication. At some level of description, at least in a theory of linguistic performance, there must be principles of language use framed in terms of notions like purpose, intention, belief, communicative act, presupposition, and so on. Nonetheless, the standard position on syntax is that its description can be given purely as a matter of linguistic form, with no use of communicative/functional terms like those just mentioned. If it should turn out that our mental representation of syntax is in terms of properties of meaning and communicative function, then the formal view of language is wrong, and over the years a number of linguists have argued for exactly this conclusion. So far, though, their arguments have not been persuasive enough to win many converts.

(6) KNOWLEDGE OF LANGUAGE ITSELF IS MODULAR. Consistent with the modular view of mind, the standard position on grammar (i.e., the mental representation of language) is that it too is subdivided into components (which, of course, may interact in complex ways in performance). To a certain extent these components correspond to the traditional division of grammatical study into phonology, lexicon, morphology, syntax and semantics. The syntactic component itself is divided into various subcomponents consisting of different sorts of rules or principles. But there is disagreement on where the boundaries are; is the passive construction, for example, best described in the lexicon, or in the syntax? If in the syntax, by base rules or transformation? Theoretical controversies of this sort are common, and can be of crucial importance, since they often relate directly to hypotheses of universal grammar.

In this view of language, then, it is the human mental representation of language—a grammar—that is the object of study. Part of the linguist's task is to infer what the form and content of this mental representation are—to construct a model of the mental representation, the linguist's grammar—and by various means to construct a theory to explain why the grammar has the properties it has, and how it could be learned, by forming a theory of the innate language faculty. But, consistent with the modular view of mind, it is assumed that the grammar does not give a complete account of linguistic behavior. Such a complete account requires understanding other parts and functions of the mind, and how they interact with knowledge of language.

1.2   Some Common Criticisms of Generative Grammar

A number of criticisms of generative grammar arise from misunderstanding its expository metaphors. Often the problem is the (mistaken) assumption that a grammar is intended as a model of the native speaker's speech processes. This is a common interpretation of generative grammar, in spite of the pains taken by Chomsky and many others to make it clear that it is not a correct interpretation. A grammar represents (or models) what native speakers know about their language that allows them to correctly pair representations of sentences with meaning representations. It is no more intended to account for how speakers actually produce sentences which they intend to convey particular notions than a theory of motion is intended as instructions for getting from Boston to Chicago. Thus, grammars are intended to represent the principles that the language learner learns, and the adult native speaker knows, which define the set of well-formed sentences of a language and associate with each sentence one or more structural descriptions. How these principles are employed in actual language use on particular occasions is not well understood, despite occasional claims to the contrary.

Critics of generative linguistics sometimes take this separation of **competence** (the principles of grammar) and **performance** (the employment of competence in the use of language) as an argument against the generative approach. Such criticisms usually involve one of five common complaints:

(1) that the identification of grammar with principles of performance is the most reasonable hypothesis *a priori*, and the burden of proof is on whoever proposes the separation of competence and performance

(2) that a distinction between competence and performance is counter-intuitive

(3) that any theory with such a separation is flawed in principle

(4) that a theory with such a distinction is *a priori* inferior to a theory without it

(5) that a theory with such a distinction necessarily fails to give a complete account of performance, therefore is incomplete, hence flawed.

Criticisms (1) through (4) are *a priori* arguments, not based on any kind of empirical consideration. We know of no reason to take any of them seriously. For the linguist, the nature of human language is a scientific question, not a philosophical one, so *a priori* arguments have little relevance. In regard to (2), even if one agrees with the judgement that the competence-performance distinction is counter-intuitive, the argument is not persuasive. Scientific theories often contain counter-intuitive hypotheses of great explanatory power. Physics is full of them. There is no reason why psychology should be free of them. Besides, it is not obvious that the present case is all that counter-intuitive, if we consider other cognitive abilities, even regarding something as unlike language as chess. Nobody would deny that most chess players learn chess by first learning the rules of chess. But the rules of chess clearly do not constitute a set of computational steps to be applied in playing chess, or instructions to the fingers for moving a particular chess piece from one place to another, let alone a strategy for winning at chess. The rules merely define possible chess moves, possible chess games, what counts as a win, a stalemate, and so on. How human players employ their knowledge of the rules in picking up and putting down pieces, evaluating moves, planning winning strategy, and so forth, is a fascinating study. But it is clear that they don't employ the rules of chess as an algorithm, as defining steps in mental computation. There is a distinction to be made between the rules of chess that every player knows, and whatever mental structures players acquire that allow them to use the rules to do the playing.

The third argument also has no force, since the question is not a matter of logic, but of fact, an important point that is often overlooked. The generative position is that the competence-performance distinction is a reflection of the structure and organization of the minds of members of a particular biological species. So it is a position on what the facts are, not a position on epistemology, logic, or other *a priori* matters. It is a position that may well be incorrect; but the only relevant objections are those that attack it as a scientific theory. There is certainly no *a priori* reason to believe that it is either more or less plausible than its opposite.

The fourth objection has no force for the same reason, since it too is an *a priori* objection, unless it is based on the proposal of a theory that is (a) as successful empirically as generative grammar but (b) does not incorporate the competence-performance distinction. So far no such theory has been proposed in any form more concrete than a wish list. There have been some vague proposals with property (b), but none that combine (a) and (b).

The fifth objection is really a restatement of the second. It too misses the point that the failure of generative grammar to give a complete account of performance is not an embarrassing oversight, but a conscious, considered position on the facts, a natural outgrowth of the modularity position, and the only relevant objection to it is one that is based on empirical evidence or on showing that there is a serious alternative theory that includes no competence-performance distinction. So far there is no such serious alternative.

Such objections may be based on the further misconception that the modularity position implies a corresponding processing order; that is, the hypothesis that grammar can be subdivided into phonology, morphology, syntax and semantics is often taken to imply that processing necessarily proceeds in a similarly compartmentalized fashion. For example, the modularity hypothesis is often taken to imply that in understanding a sentence the mind first carries out a complete phonological analysis, which in turn provides input to morphological processing, that in turn to syntactic processing, and the complete syntactic analysis is performed before any semantic analysis begins. This **bottom-up** view of things is certainly counter-intuitive and implausible (though it could conceivably turn out to be correct), but that is irrelevant, since it is in fact not implied by the modular view of language. Just how the various modules interact in performance is an open empirical question, and in the absence of a theory of exactly how they interact, and how the mind works, questions of computational simplicity are irrelevant. And if it should turn out (as we suspect it will) that modules interact in very complex non-bottom-up ways in processing, it would not be a disconfirmation of the modularity hypothesis: modularity does not imply bottom-up processing.

In sum, the position embodied in the competence-performance distinction is not a matter of logic but of what the biological and psychological facts are, and *a priori* arguments are irrelevant. There is nothing illogical, incoherent, or even implausible about the distinction, though it is certainly possible that it will turn out to be wrong. But that has not yet been shown.

1.3   Pernicious Metaphors

From its earliest days, the exposition of generative grammar has been permeated with metaphors that represent it in terms of procedures. These have misled generations of students into believing it is something it is not, nor was ever intended to be.

The granddaddy of them all is the central term **generate**. Borrowed from a metaphorical use in mathematics, this term means no more (and no less) than 'describe', 'define', 'give an explicit account of' or 'analyze'. Thus the formula for the graph of a circle:

$$(x-a)^2 + (y-b)^2 = c^2$$

generates (i.e., describes) a set of circles in a plane defined by the x and y axes, a potentially infinite set, depending on the values assigned to a and b. Construing the formula this way, it says that certain objects, ones fitting the formula, are circles, and (implicitly) everything else is not. The formula is not a circle-producing machine; it doesn't produce circles, it only defines them.

Likewise, a grammar is just a set of statements that define a set, possibly infinite, of sentences of some language.[1] We say that the grammar generates that set of sentences, but by that we don't mean that it is a device for producing sentences. Nonetheless, many novices in the field labor for some time, consciously or unconsciously, under the false impression that a generative grammar is a model of a sentence-producing device, and are often dismayed at the idea of surface filters, which they understand as jettisoning a derivation on the basis of some property of the final form in the derivation. Their dismay is based on the feeling that it is somehow inefficient to go to all the work of building up a derivation according to the rules of the grammar, only to have the whole business discarded due to some surface filter. But this feeling comes from confusing *grammar* and *algorithm*, and on a thorough misunderstanding of what a classical phrase-structure derivation in a transformational grammar is: it is not a set of processes, but a set of abstract relations, more like the definition of a circle. There is no work involved, and no implication that anyone or anything actually builds up derivations and then throws them out; the only claim is that the derivation is not one that represents the structural description of a well-formed sentence of the language.

It is no wonder that such misinterpretations are common, because there is a whole host of metaphors that syntacticians have used that reinforce this kind of mistaken interpretation. They have talked about a transformation (itself a pernicious metaphor) "applying" to a phrase-marker, to "change" it into another, of a rule "operating" on some structure as "input", "to yield" some other structure as "ouput". They have used action nominalizations to speak of the transformational "operations" of deletion, insertion, and substitution as processes. They talked about the way a transformational rule relates one phrase-marker to another as a "structural change". All of these metaphors

---

[1] Syntactic theories that are of any interest at all also assign structural descriptions to the sentences they generate; that does not affect the point we are making here.

imply that the objects being related are concrete objects that exist in time, and have a spatial orientation to boot. Talking about "leftward movement" and the "right-hand" side of a rule is only an abbreviatory convention that takes advantage of our (arbitrary) Western convention of writing from left to right, but it reinforces the mistaken notion that syntactic derivations, like phrase-markers, are spatially oriented objects, built up by a grammar, when in actuality they are merely statements of relation and category membership of syntactic structures.

In addition, the term *derivation* has been used in a way that implies that strings or phrase-markers are derived from strings or other phrase-markers (or in unforgivably sloppy expositions, that sentences are derived from other sentences), and that there is an orientation (usually from deep to surface structure) to transformational derivations. But nothing could be farther from the intended meaning of *derivation*, as stressed by both Chomsky (1971) and Lakoff (1971). A transformational derivation is simply an ordered[2] set of phrase markers

$$<P_0, ..., P_n >$$

such that P_0 is the structure generated by the base rules and P_n is the surface structure, and for every pair $<P_i, P_{i+1} >$ in the derivation, there is a transformational rule saying exactly how P_i and P_{i+1} correspond; for a derivation to be well-formed, all such pairs must be well-formed. For example, the topicalization rule needed to describe sentences like *Beans, he won't eat* can be seen as a rule that says that if a derivation contains two adjacent structures that are identical except that some NP with certain characteristics is embedded within P_i, while in P_{i+1} the corresponding NP is Chomsky-adjoined to the left of some S it is embedded in, then the pair P_i, P_{i+1} is well formed. Thus, transformations define classes of well-formed pairs of phrase-markers in derivations, and have a **filtering** function in excluding from the set of derivations describing the sentences of the language, all possible derivations with ordered pairs of phrase-markers which do not meet the conditions of some licensing rule or rules.

Derivations do not exist in time or space, so such notions as the beginning or end of a derivation, and the direction of a derivation (from deep to surface, or vice versa) are simply meaningless, except as metaphors for more correct (and less intuitive) mathematical notions. A derivation is a logically ordered set of relations $<<x_i, x_j >, <x_j, x_k >, ... <x_m, x_n >>$, not a process. As a consequence, claims to the effect that properties of surface structure play

---

[2]Ordered only in a logical sense, e.g., the non-spatial, non-temporal sense invoked in set theory; these metaphors are ubiquitous.

a distinctive role in determining the semantic representation (where semantic representation is a stage in a derivation) are entirely equivalent to claims that properties of semantic representation play a distinctive role in determining properties of surface structure. Both say only that there is a significant relationship between semantic representation and surface structure—hardly a novel idea. Neither says anything about how speakers produce sentences; it remains an entirely open question how grammars are utilized in the production and comprehension of language.

Given the correct understanding of what a derivation is, the following dictum, commonly invoked in the 1960s and 1970s, is meaningless:

"Transformations cannot/do not/should not change meaning."

The idea of a meaning *changing* within a derivation is completely incoherent. A single derivation relates one surface structure to one meaning (strictly: to one semantic representation). The intended sense of the injunction is just this: if two sentences have the same deep structure, then they must have the same semantic representation.[3] If the meaning that informants impute to a surface structure does not match the meaning assigned to it by the grammar, it means that the grammar has incorrectly assigned the meaning (or the surface structure), not that it has changed the meaning.

We have mentioned some of the metaphors that (misleadingly) imply that a derivation is a process. Many of them further (and perhaps more misleadingly) imply that the process is a controlled and manipulated one. Inferences along these lines arise from the mistaken notion that a grammar generates sentences in more or less the same way that General Motors manufactures automobiles. Not only do we find linguists saying that some rule operates or applies, we find some saying things like "we [linguists? speakers? grammar-operators?] apply Rule X to derive Phrase-marker$_n$ ..." or "we must apply Raising before Passive to get the correct result" and so on. This implies a model of the grammar as a sentence-producing machine, as if one dropped in a nickel and a sentence popped out below.

The notion of a rule of grammar under this interpretation of what a grammar is is equally distorted. The term *rule* gets misinterpreted as 'injunction':

"Move an NP from after V to subject position."
"Move anything."

---

[3]Not all linguists held this position; Chomsky (1971) and Jackendoff (1972), for example, did not. The converse, that if two surface structures have the same meaning, they must have the same deep structure, does not hold, by the way: they might have non-identical, but semantically equivalent semantic representations.

or process:

"A post-verbal NP becomes the subject of that verb."
"Anything moves anywhere."

or (especially pernicious) as a tool:

"We can then use Passive to put the NP in subject position."
"We can then use Move-Alpha to move the NP into a governed
position."

But it has always been the case that the intended sense of *rule of gram-mar* is simply 'statement of regularity': a transformational derivation was well-formed if the members of every pair of phrase-markers adjacent in the derivation were related by some rule of grammar, that is, if some specified relationship held between them. Thus, a so-called "NP-movement rule" merely says that two adjacent phrase-markers in a derivation are a well-formed pair if they are identical except that in one there is an NP in a certain position, and in the other there is no NP in that position, but there is a corresponding NP in some other (specified) position. Unfortunately, most linguists use the misleading metaphorical abbreviations without thinking about them. It is worth the effort not to use them.

The notion that transformational rules are "obligatory" or "optional" also reinforces the incorrect notion that rules are processes. When we say that a certain rule is obligatory, we don't mean that some process must change some phrase-marker in some way, but rather, that if a derivation contains a phrase-marker that meets the structural description of that rule, then the derivation will be well-formed ONLY IF some phrase-marker with that description is adjacent in the derivation to a phrase-marker corresponding in the way specified in the rule.

When we say that a certain rule is optional, we don't mean that a linguist or language-user can freely choose to exploit it or not, but rather that a pair of phrase-markers is well-formed IF the first meets the structural description of the rule, and the adjacent phrase-marker corresponds to it in the specified way. If every pair is well-formed, then the derivation is well-formed. But a derivation which is identical, *mutatis mutandis*, except that it does not contain any pair described by that rule will also be well-formed.

In fact, a speaker's choice of sentence form may be influenced by any of a number of matters, both syntactic and non-syntactic (see Chapter 2, Section 3 for some relevant discussion). For example, Extraposition has been described in terms of an optional transformation, which is to say that two derivations that differ only in whether Extraposition relates two adjacent phrase-markers in it are, all other things being equal, both well-formed derivations. But a derivation in which Extraposition relates two adjacent phrase-markers may nonetheless either entail or preclude violation of some other principle, for example a surface filter (see Ross 1967 for some examples).

Likewise, a transformation could be syntactically optional, yet make a difference in appropriateness. For example, Topicalization is commonly considered to be an optional transformation. But topicalized sentences are subtly different from their non-topicalized counterparts in discourse appropriateness. The difference has to do with poorly understood matters of topicality, focus, and contrast (cf. Ward 1985), as illustrated in examples like the following, where uttering (1) suggests that there are people the speaker is crazy about, while uttering (2) lacks this suggestion.

1. This man I'm not crazy about.
2. I'm not crazy about this man.

As a consequence, even though the transformation involved is optional, the speaker's choice between the two is not free,[4] but depends on subtle matters of discourse context. This does not constitute evidence against the claim that Topicalization is optional, since optionality is a purely syntactic notion having to do with syntactic well-formedness; it has no implications whatever concerning free choice in performance.

A more helpful model of a rule of grammar might be that of a filter or sieve: a grammar is a (complex) set of well-formedness conditions (on underlying structures, derivations, surface structures, or whatever). These conditions distinguish derivations or structures that describe sentences of the language, from potential (but ill-formed) ones that don't. Indeed, various components of the grammar have been spoken of as filters since at least 1965 (Chomsky 1965, McCawley 1968a, Perlmutter 1971, Chomsky and Lasnik 1977). The notion that the grammar as a whole should be considered a sort of filter has gained widespread acceptance, and is explicit in Generalized Phrase-Structure Grammar (GPSG) and Head-Driven Phrase-Structure Grammar (HPSG). But even as this conception becomes more commonplace, there will be those who will want to understand filters as culling machines, and we will again have to wrestle with metaphorical interpretations of *grammar* as a device which a speaker operates in order to talk.

---

[4]We don't mean to imply a stricture on free will, only that choosing to say one sentence instead of the other may lead to misunderstanding, like any other violation of the ground rules for rational discourse. Speakers are of course free to speak in knowing inconsistency with such rules, but at a cost. To know the rules is to know the cost.

In any case, all of the following expressions and constructions contribute to the misunderstandings fostered by describing relations in procedural terms, and it is a useful exercise to scrupulously avoid them.

- CONSTRUCTION METAPHORS: *produce, make, build, procedure, process, level*; purpose infinitive

- REWRITING METAPHORS: *rewrite to, go to, replace, derive*

- TRANSFORMATION METAPHORS: *change, transform, render, turn NP into, copy, delete, insert, add, move, put, invert, re-order, mark, "star"*

- OPERATION METAPHORS: *return, yield, give, input, output, operate, apply, use, assign*

- TEMPORAL METAPHORS: *then, next, later, after, before; beginning, end*; perfect aspect

It is actually surprisingly easy to reframe such descriptions in more declarative terms with such expressions as: *correspond, consist of, contain, instantiate, license, allow, describe* and *be*.

2   TOPICS AND HYPOTHESES

The purpose of this chapter is to draw out and make explicit what working syntacticians know but rarely discuss. The basic principles of the analytic enterprise that are explicated here, and the principles of assembling and presenting arguments for or against particular hypotheses (i.e., evidence) that are the subject of Chapter 3 should not vary from one framework to another; what varies and changes is 1) particular assumptions about various phenomena, 2) assumptions about the inventory of elements supposed to be universal, and 3) the importance attached to particular assumptions. The approach to analysis and argumentation presented here is appropriate to any syntactic theory, indeed to most rational inquiry.

2.1   The Problem of Grammatical Analysis

There are two sorts of activities that syntacticians engage in. One is the construction and evaluation of syntactic theories at a fairly abstract level, independent of detailed analyses of particular languages. There are a number of linguists who do this, some who do it exclusively. The second sort of activity that engages syntacticians is detailed grammatical analysis of data from one or more languages, sometimes for the purpose of testing predictions of some syntactic theory or hypothesis, but sometimes for purposes of description. In practice, the two sorts of activities are interdependent: it is impossible to articulate a description of a language without making some assumptions about what languages are like (that is, without adopting some syntactic theory), and it is impossible to test a theory of what languages are like without examining particular languages in detail. Likewise, it is impossible to argue for the correctness of an analysis without making some assumptions, which constitute a minimal theory.

The problem of learning to do syntactic analysis, then, is not so much a matter of learning a theory and techniques for describing new bodies of data in the terms it defines, as it is a matter of learning how to test and compare analyses, in order to be able to demonstrate reasons to accept one's own analysis. (The criteria and values that govern this enterprise are the subject of Chapter 3.)

In addition, there is still another task to be faced and mastered: the problem of presenting the analysis and accompanying arguments in such a fashion that other scholars will understand the analysis and be persuaded by the arguments for it. This is not a trivial problem, and it is addressed in Chapter 4.

Summing up, there are four kinds of skills that must be brought to bear in syntactic analysis:

(1) Understanding the conceptual foundations of syntactic theory, and the principles and formalisms of particular theories.

(2) The skills of doing syntactic analysis: experience at doing analysis, knowing what kinds of things to expect, and various rules of thumb, heuristics, and other tricks of the trade.

(3) The skills necessary for constructing arguments that support your analysis as opposed to other possible analyses.

(4) The skills necessary for presenting your analysis, and the arguments for it, in the most transparent fashion possible, so that the reader will see immediately the structure of both without any need for exegesis, and with a minimum likelihood of misinterpretation.

The rest of this chapter and the two following it are devoted to discussion of analysis, argumentation, and presentation. It is assumed here that the reader has a reasonable understanding of the principles and of the conceptual foundations of one or more syntactic theories, and that what is important now is putting them to use in doing and reporting research.

2.2   Finding an Analysis: Questions and Answers

There is no fool-proof, theory-independent recipe for isolating a tractable set of facts to analyze, and no algorithm for deducing an analysis from them. Some students may conceive of the problem in this way, but that puts the cart before the horse: research is typically theory-driven, not data-driven, and starts with a universal hypothesis, i.e., a hypothesis about some potentially infinite domain, not with a circumscribed set of data. What will be considered a reasonable analysis depends on what assumptions are made, about the framework of grammatical description (the details of the syntactic theory that is adopted), and about the structure of the language(s) being analyzed (i.e., about aspects of the grammar of the language(s) that are presupposed by but not part of the analysis at issue). Since both of these sets of assumptions are constantly subject to change, it would be futile, even counterproductive, to try to stipulate beforehand a set of assumptions from which analyses of arbitrary linguistic data could be deduced. It would also be misleading, since it would imply that the analysis is always lurking in the facts, waiting for the right techniques to uncover it, whereas in fact, hypotheses with the potential to explain data come from outside it, and it does not matter from where, or by what means (cf. Popper 1968).

Since beginners seem to have more trouble getting started doing analysis, testing hypotheses, and getting out of dead ends, this section concentrates on those issues, rather than on hypothesis formation,.

2.2.1 Finding a Suitable Topic: What Do You Want to Know, and Why Do You Want to Know It?

Beginning students are sometimes discouraged by the belief that "all the easy stuff's already been done. What's left is really hard." But when that "easy stuff," is examined closely, it often turns out that it is only half-done, and that the conclusions do not follow from the premises (which often are not made explicit), or that the assumptions they are based on are no longer considered tenable. A surprising amount of the "easy stuff" needs to be re-done. In fact, of course, there is no truly easy stuff, and never was. What looks easy often does so only because the writer does not mention the facts that reveal its full complexity.

Suppose you know that something interests you, but do not know quite how to get started. Chances are the topic you have identified is only broadly defined in your conscious mind—an area of syntax, a certain language, but no specific questions. This reflects a common misconception that researchers begin by choosing a topic. Probably it is the other way around: researchers find themselves interested in a topic because they have questions about the relations it embraces. A major factor in successful research is choosing what question to tackle. (Insofar as reading on a topic is a form of background research, it is just as futile to read without a clear question to provide a purpose for the reading as it is to try to say something original and relevant without considering what needs to be known, and why it needs to be known.)

A good technique for isolating a problem you can handle in the time you have is to begin by stating precisely what you want to know; for example, by making a list (the longer the better) of all the SPECIFIC questions (the more specific the better) concerning this topic that you would like to know the answer to, assuming that you have one or more languages and one or more syntactic theories in mind. After all, chances are, if there is a "topic" you know you are interested in, it is because you suppose that certain facts relating to it provide either counterexamples or corroboration to some salient claim or assumption. It is important to formulate the items on your list as questions, not noun phrases. Posing a question projects a set of potential answers, but a noun phrase does not project any researchable hypotheses, only confusion.

The types of questions that papers and articles successfully address include:

1. (How) can such-and-such a phenomenon in language L be insightfully described in theory X?
2. Why are certain instances of a certain construction considered unacceptable by speakers?
3. Can the answer to (2) be accounted for within theory X?
4. If the answer to (3) is 'no', what kind of theory of syntax would be able to predict the answer to (2)?
5. Should the answer to (2) be accounted for within theory X?
6. Can the standard analysis of this construction in theory X be shown to be incorrect?
7. If the answer to (6) is 'yes', what are the implications for an opposing theory Y?
8. Both Hypothesis P and Hypothesis Q are possible accounts of this phenomenon within theory Y. Do P and Q differ in their predictions? If so, how?

If you can relax and allow yourself to give concrete articulations to the questions lurking within your interest in a topic, you will have a sizable list of questions, and may be concerned that they cannot all be satisfactorily addressed in the time or space allotted to you. This abundance invites you to limit yourself to a smaller topic, and you now have in front of you a sizable list of more specific questions from which to choose. The obvious next step is to examine these questions and determine, for each one, or for the ones you find most interesting, what you would have to do to obtain a satisfactory answer.

In choosing a research question, there are three matters to consider; failing to consider them increases the possibility that you will discover too late that your question is not answerable.

1. *Why do you want to know the answer to this question?* Why should anyone care what the answer is? There are at least two potential benefits to taking this matter seriously. First, in attempting to articulate a rationale for pursuing the question, you may discover that it is not exactly the question you want to investigate, and this may lead you to formulate a more interesting and/or more tractable question to work on. Second, when you succeed in articulating a satisfactory rationale, you will have the core of the introduction

to your paper, where you lay out for the reader the question and a discussion of its importance.

2. *What propositions does the QUESTION commit you to assuming?* What does the question presuppose? What do you have to take for granted if this question is to be answerable? What has to be defined before you can evaluate (or maybe even formulate) potential answers to this question? Obviously, if you discover that the question presupposes something that you have reason to believe is not correct, it will not be a good question for you to try to answer, and you will want to reformulate it so that it does not require you to (pretend to) accept something you doubt. Or perhaps this discovery will move you to change your project to evaluating the validity of the suspect presupposition. Likewise, if you discover that you need to define a notion for which a satisfactory definition does not yet exist, in order to describe the ontological commitments of the question, that may make it less attractive. At the same time, it raises the question of obtaining a satisfactory definition as a relevant and important question in itself, and therefore, a possible paper topic. Just RECOGNIZING the ontological commitments of your question is not the neverending task that defending them is, and when they are explicit, it saves a lot of time in the event that you discover that the answer you favor makes contradictory predictions (cf. Chapter 3).

3. *What will count as an answer?* If this is very hard to answer, try reformulating the question. If the set of possible answers is not finite and small (like the set consisting of 'yes' and 'no'), then the question is too large or too vague to expect to be able to answer in a semester or two; it needs to be narrowed down until it has a small and definite set of potential answers. If you formulated your question with a particular answer in mind, make things easy on yourself, and reformulate your question as a polar ("yes-no") question about the hypothesis that that answer represents. There is no particular virtue in pretending not to have an opinion, and it may work against articulating the most specific and easily tested hypothesis possible.

Now, supposing that you have one or more research questions, and know what the possible answers to each are, it is useful to determine, for each possible answer, what would force you to accept that answer as correct. In general terms, what would the world have to be like for that to be the right answer? And following through, what specific evidence would enable you to prefer one answer over all the others: what kinds of judgements on what sorts of sentences would force you to conclude that that answer was correct to the exclusion of the others? Once you know this, you have, *ipso facto*, the beginnings of a structured, detailed research plan laid out before you. The hardest part is now done.

It may be instructive to see how this works with a hypothetical example. Suppose the question you have picked from your list looks like a fairly specific one: "To what extent can that theory account for this construction in that language?" Before you go any further, it pays to consider whether this is really the question you want to try to answer. What exactly are you trying to get at? Is (A) what you really want to know? Or are you more specifically interested in (B)? Or is (C) what you're really interested in?

A. Is the theory a good theory?
B. Does this construction of that language falsify some basic principle of the theory?
C. What is the best account of the construction that the theory provides? How good is it?

Questions like (A) are of course what drives research in the first place, but it is clear that since *good* is a relative term (good for what? good at what?), just having an answer to (A) as phrased is not very informative. Getting an answer to (B) would provide important information for evaluating Theory T, but it is considerably narrower than the question as originally phrased; it does not say anything about what insight into that construction Theory T might offer. And (C) sounds considerably more ambitious than the original question, as it appears to involve two distinct open-ended evaluations, not a simple yes-no discrimination.

For the moment, let us entertain all three questions as potential research questions. Regardless of which is chosen, the reason for interest is the same: Theory T is an influential theory; it is important to know if it makes incorrect predictions, so that it can be improved, or abandoned in favor of a better theory.

When we examine the propositions that asking the various alternative questions presuppose, we can see that all three versions make the same presuppositions. They presuppose that there is some particular construction which is unique, that instances of it are identifiable, and that there is a set of assumptions and principles that are identifiable as constituting the theory. In all three cases, it is incumbent on the researcher to describe exactly what the properties of the construction are, providing evidence that that description is correct, and what principles and assumptions of the theory are relevant to the investigation.

Questions (A–C) differ, of course, in what they define as counting as an answer. Alternatives (A) and (B) are yes-no questions. The possible answers are members of the set {yes, no}, or maybe the set {yes, no, it is impossible to say}. Alternative (C), on the other hand, is two questions and requires two different kinds of answers. The answer to *What is the best account of the construction that the theory provides?* will be some account from the possibly infinite set $\{a_1, a_2, a_3, ...\}$ of descriptions consistent with the theory. The answer to *How good is it?* will be a rating on some arbitrary scale, say, a value somewhere between 1 and 10 on a scale from 1 to 10. This makes answering (C) look like a lot more work than answering (B).

In order to look for an answer to any question in an efficient fashion, it is necessary to know for each potential answer, what would force you to accept that answer. In the case of alternative (A), *Is the theory a good theory?*, the evidence supporting an affirmative answer would be evidence that it makes all the right predictions for all known languages. Conversely, a negative answer would be forced by evidence that it makes demonstrably incorrect predictions. Clearly, the search for evidence forcing an affirmative answer is not a practical research program, but this is not so for the negative: learning that the construction falsified some basic principle of the theory would be evidence that the theory was not so good. And evidence for that would be evidence that the best analysis of the construction must either make incorrect predictions about sentences of the language, or violate some principle of the theory. The opposite conclusion, that the construction does not falsify any basic principle of the theory, would be forced by evidence that there are analyses of it which are consistent with the principles of the theory which make no obvious false predictions and require no special amendments to the theory. That is, a demonstration that a single analysis of the construction consistent with previously articulated principles of the theory accounts for the properties of the construction would constitute a negative answer to (B). Discovering the best account of the construction that the theory provides would require finding, for one of the potential accounts allowed by the theory, evidence that it makes fewer false predictions than any other member of the set and/or requires fewer auxiliary hypotheses relating to the theory. Evaluating how good that best account is requires evaluating the consequences of any false predictions it makes compared to accounts of the construction framed in other theories. Thus, it turns out that supporting an affirmative answer to (B), which looked like a nice, simple question, with a yes-no answer, actually entails answering the open-ended (C), a task which one might expect not to be able to make much headway on in a semester. This does not mean that the question must be abandoned. Looking at the characterizations of what would have to be determined suggests an answerable reformulation:

D. Making only standard assumptions and supported additions, what must an analysis of this construction look like in terms of that theory? Does it make correct predictions about sentences of this language?

This is not quite A, B, or C, but it significantly narrows down the field of inquiry for pursuing them later, and answering it will suggest directions to be pursued in other research.

2.2.2 Testing Specific Hypotheses

A commonly encountered sub-problem in grammatical description is to figure out the principle governing the distribution of some expression or type of construction. That is, in the course of testing some claim or other, it must be explained why certain asterisked sentences are unacceptable, while others (unasterisked) are acceptable. If the framework chosen does not immediately suggest a hypothesis, it often helps to take a small amount of data, and look for patterns from which you can predict which sentences will be acceptable. For example, you may notice that in all of the acceptable examples, and none of the unacceptable ones, the verb is finite, or the subject and direct object agree in person, number, and gender. If no hypothesis about the principle determining the distribution occurs to you, it may be useful to expand the data, for example, by constructing sentences containing the form or construction in question, varying one syntactic property of the sentence at a time, and determining whether the resultant expressions are acceptable or not. Before long, at least one hypothesis will occur to you that will predict the patterns of acceptability that you note.

Wherever the hypothesis comes from, the next step is to test it. This means first, determining what predictions it makes BEYOND THE SET OF FACTS IT WAS DESIGNED TO EXPLAIN, and then, evaluating those predictions by constructing (a) sentences of the form it predicts will be acceptable which are as different as possible from the ones which provoked it, but still in conformity with it, and also (b) sentences of the form it predicts will be unacceptable. The sentences you use to test the predictions of the hypothesis should be as similar as possible to exemplars already known to be acceptable—you are looking for the syntactic counterpart of the phonological minimal pair, sentences which differ in only one respect from a sentence known to be acceptable, and differ in a respect which is identified by the hypothesis as criterial. Determine (empirically) which sentences are acceptable: ask a native speaker whom you can trust to understand what kind of information you are seeking—often you can act as your own informant. If the judgements correspond to the predictions of your hypothesis, fine; your hypothesis is corroborated. If not, you need to devise a hypothesis that predicts these data as well as the previously examined sentences. Deduce what additional predictions this new hypothesis makes, and construct sentences to test if those predictions are correct, and so on, until you are satisfied that the predictions your eventual hypothesis makes are in fact borne out. Whenever acceptability judgements on sentences contradict your hypothesis rather than supporting it, try a different hypothesis, until you find one that accounts for all the data you have accumulated in this fashion.

You will need to expand the data not just to look for a hypothesis, but to test your hypothesis, once you have one. There are lots of ways to do this expansion—for example, changing the tense, mood, and subject (person, number, animateness, definiteness, etc.) of a clause; putting the expression in question into a subordinate clause (differentiating among complement, relative, and adverbial clauses at least) if it is given in a main clause, and vice versa; changing the grammatical relations (subject, object, etc.) of nominal expressions; substituting different main verbs; negating, questioning; and so forth, as relevant. For example, faced with the hypothesis that the phrasal verb *bug off* is restricted to appearing in imperatives, as an account of the difference in acceptability between (1a) and (1b), one would systematically examine the effect of changes in tense and mood, as in (2) , and in person, as in (3).[1]

    1a. Bug off.
    1b. *He bugged off.

    2a. Will you bug off?
    2b. Let him bug off!
    2c. He will bug off.
    2d. You bug off.
    2e. You bug off, don't you?

    3a. You bugged off.
    3b. Will they bug off?
    3b. I bug off.

If that investigation proved inconclusive, one might expand the data systematically by varying verb form (4), embeddedness (5), and polarity (6).

    4a. You/he ought to bug off.
    4b. You/he must bug off.
    4c. You/They were bugging off.

    5a. To bug off/Bugging off is risky.
    5b. We told you/him to bug off.

---

[1]As (2-6) are constructed test sentences, they are not accompanied by annotations of acceptability.

5c. It's essential that you/he bug off.

5d. We regret that you/he bug off.

5e. Although/If you/they bug off, things will be easier.

5f. There will be rewards for you/those who bug off.

5g. You/Those who bug off should sit in aisle seats.

6a. Don't bug off.

6b. We insist that you not bug off.

Changes of this sort should become second nature to you.

A caveat: do not confuse the process of finding an adequate hypothesis with what you need to say to present support for it. There is no reason to drag your reader down all the blind alleys you traversed before finding a satisfactory hypothesis. Present only your best statement of the solution, and present all and only the data that are relevant to motivating it.

2.2.3   Choosing Among Potential Solutions

Choosing among potential solutions is just a variation on finding a solution: you need to deduce the predictions of each candidate hypothesis that distinguish it from the others, and determine which predictions are borne out. Often it makes the logic of your argument considerably clearer to compare your hypothesis to a null hypothesis—a hypothesis that does not make the substantive claim of your hypothesis, but is otherwise the same. (See Chapter 3, Sections 6 and 7, for further discussion.)

2.2.4   How To Cope When Things Go Wrong

If all of the analyses you can devise for some phenomenon you must analyze are unsatisfactory, all is not lost. Pick the most nearly adequate of them, and write out what it does right, say why, and show how. Then show what it fails to account for, and say why and show how it fails. Often just laying out the problem in this fashion is enough to suggest a more adequate treatment. Often it will point you to an assumption that perhaps you did not realize you were making; your eventual solution may involve abandoning that assumption. In the event that you are not led to a more adequate solution, you have still made a contribution, in showing that an apparently promising solution will not in fact work, given certain assumptions which, presumably, you have made explicit.

Likewise, if you need to show how certain assumptions lead to a certain conclusion (for example, if you have to show how certain principles provide an analysis of some sentence), and you cannot, try as you might, get those assumptions or principles to yield that conclusion, try to explain, in writing, why they will not give the proposed result. As with the previous situation, the process of explaining may make explicit an error in your logic, or an extraneous assumption in your reasoning, or even in the question itself. Even if it does not, your explanation should give a concise, explicit account of the problem, and by virtue of that, call into question the consistency of the relevant assumptions with each other. This too contributes to the advancement of knowledge (cf. Popper 1968).

2.3 Non-syntactic Explanations for Apparently Syntactic Facts

For the most part, the discussion of syntactic analysis has so far not been specific to syntax, or even to linguistics. But one of the tasks and responsibilities of the syntactician is to provide a theory of syntax which describes all and only the possible natural language syntaxes, and this requires being able to distinguish syntactic phenomena from other phenomena, perhaps linguistic, perhaps extra-linguistic, which may impinge on the distribution of syntactic forms. Because phenomena don't present themselves sorted into syntactic and non-syntactic kinds, this section seeks to clarify the distinction between syntactic and non-syntactic explanations for apparently syntactic facts, and then to describe briefly, and with examples, some of the kinds of apparently syntactic phenomena for which non-syntactic descriptions and explanations might be offered.

To begin with, what are "apparently syntactic facts"? Syntactic facts are facts which are properly described in terms of syntactic relations (such as precede, dominate, subject-of) among syntactic elements (such as constituent, category type, NP). Apparently-syntactic facts are facts which apparently are properly described in syntactic terms. A syntactic explanation for such facts is one which itself uses exclusively syntactic terms to account for why those facts are as they are, and not some other way.

For example,[2] the claim that sentences that include the NP *a damn thing* are grammatical only if a negative precedes *a damn thing* apparently refers to a syntactic fact. The claim that the clause in which *a damn thing* occurs has to refer to a proposition toward which the speaker has a negative attitude does not apparently refer to a syntactic fact. Describing some sentence as unacceptable because the subject and verb do not agree claims that the unacceptability is a

---

[2] In the examples to follow, we use the terms *fact* and *explanation* advisedly. No claim is made or implied that "facts" referred to in examples are correctly described, or that "explanations" offered are empirically corroborated or even entirely coherent.

result of syntactic facts. Claiming that a sentence is unacceptable because it is silly, contradictory, false, or improbable does not refer to syntactic properties, and thus does not refer to an apparently syntactic fact. Some more examples: the observation that "the underlying subject of an imperative sentence is a second person NP" is an apparently syntactic fact. The observation that "the understood subject of an imperative sentence refers to the addressee of the sentence" is not apparently a syntactic fact. The claim that "the passive transformation allows an underlying direct object NP to appear as a subject because Passive is a cyclic rule and all cyclic rules change grammatical relations" would be a syntactic explanation for an apparently syntactic fact, as is the claim that Passive has this property because it allows the underlying direct object to appear in the position where subjects normally appear. But the claim that "the understood subject of an imperative is a second person pronoun because second person NPs refer to the addressee of an utterance and you can't order people to do something unless you're talking to them" would be a non-syntactic explanation for an apparently syntactic fact.

It should be clear that the difference between what we are calling facts and what we are calling explanations is merely a matter of the level at which an account is offered for some phenomenon: the theory which explains some fact at one level is itself a fact to be explained by a higher-level theory.

The most nearly syntactic sort of non-syntactic explanation for apparently syntactic phenomena is morphological explanation. An example of a morphological explanation for a syntactic fact would be a claim that some particular phrase could only occur in sentences where it did not have to be inflected (e.g., for case, number, tense, etc.). Data like the following might suggest such an explanation.

1a. Beware of the dog.
1b. *I'm bewaring of the dog.
1c. He was told to beware of the dog.
1d. *He bewore of the dog.
1e. It's essential that he beware of the dog.

Other morphological explanations might refer to the presence of a particular inflection or other morpheme (cf. Perlmutter 1971, Ross 1972b).

Another commonly encountered kind of non-syntactic explanation for apparently syntactic phenomena is pragmatic explanation. A description or explanation for some ostensibly syntactic phenomenon is characterized as pragmatic if it refers at any point to the USE of the linguistic expression rather than to its form. A description is pragmatic if it refers to facts about the context, including facts about the speaker of the sentence, such as her attitudes, beliefs, and intentions. Many descriptive predicates commonly assumed to be part of the vocabulary of syntactic description refer in fact to pragmatic notions— notions that concern not the form of a sentence, but its use. Coreference, for example, is not a property of noun phrases in a sentence like (2).

2. John thinks he is smart.

Rather, coreference is a property of relations assumed (by the speaker) to hold between the utterances of two or more NPs and some real or imagined entity. In particular, it is the property of sameness of assumed intended reference: the speaker may be assumed to intend the utterances of the NPs to be understood as referring to the same entity. Reference itself, as this discussion makes evident, is a pragmatic notion: NPs do not refer all by themselves. Speakers refer to entities by uttering NPs with the intention that they (the speakers) will be understood to be referring to those entities. Words like *intention*, *infer*, *attitude*, *belief*, *refer*, and *utterance* in a description are always a dead giveaway that the phenomenon is being described as regulated by a pragmatic principle.

Another example of a phenomenon that has seen confusion of syntactic and pragmatic descriptions involves imperatives. The term *imperative*, referring to a certain class of grammatical forms is usually used to express a syntactic (or morphological) notion; but the terms *command, order,* and *request* are generally pragmatic: they are used to refer to an assumption, an intention, and an attitude on the part of a speaker in saying something to an addressee.

Thus, all of the sentences in (3) can be commands, because they can all be rationally used with the intention of letting an addressee know that the speaker wants the addressee to perform (or arrange for the performance of) the action referred to, but only (3a) is an imperative.

3a. Feed the cat.
3b. Would you feed the cat.
3c. I'd like you to feed the cat.
3d. Why don't you feed the cat.
3e. Let the cat be fed.
3f. The cat shall be fed.

We will give one more example of a pragmatic description for an ostensibly syntactic phenomenon before moving on to other kinds of nonsyntactic accounts. Recall that the data in (1) suggested that the distribution of the form *beware* was regulated by a morphological criterion: it could only occur if it was uninflected. The data in (4) suggest that this criterion, while not utterly false, is insufficient.

4a. I want you to beware of the dog.
4b. *They won't beware of the dog.
4c. I'll warn them to beware of the dog.
4d. *They expect to beware of the dog.

The word *beware* is not inflected in any of these sentences, but (4b) and (4d) are considered unacceptable nonetheless. Perhaps the factor determining acceptability is pragmatic: *beware* is used in (4a) and (4c), as well as in the acceptable examples in (1), as, or to refer to, a warning to the referent of the understood subject of *beware* to watch out. The unacceptable sentences in (1), and (4b) and (4d) do not refer to warnings, and would not be used with any other verb (like *watch out*) to convey or describe warnings to the entity that corresponds to the subject of the verb *beware*. It might be suggested that the pragmatic explanation makes the morphological explanation superfluous. If this were the case, one would expect that sentences like those in (5) would be acceptable, because they refer to conveying warnings, even though they are inflected. However, such sentences are in fact unacceptable.

5a. *I told you you should have beworn/bewared of the dog.
5b. *You ought to be bewaring of the dog.

It may not be obvious how the data in (4) suggest the conclusion that the distribution of *beware* is governed by a pragmatic principle referring to warning. Here, as elsewhere, the best test for pragmatic regulation is asking, "What kind of situation would we have to imagine in order for the relevant unacceptable examples to be acceptable?" If there is no way that the relevant aspects of the world could be, short of being such that the English language works differently from the way it now clearly works, then the criterion determining the unacceptability of the examples is syntactic or lexical, part of the grammar. If you can describe a way that the world could be (and this includes beliefs or intentions that the speaker and/or intended audience must be assumed to have) which would make the examples appropriate to use, then one would want the grammar to claim that they were grammatical, and the criterion determining their acceptability must be pragmatically extragrammatical. Your description of the way the world would have to be should provide a clue as to what the property of the unacceptable examples is that makes them unacceptable. In the case of (4a), if we understand it as a description of a wish or an attitude, it is as unacceptable as (4b) or (4d), but if we imagine it being used to warn someone about a dog, it is perfectly fine. Thus, the relevance of the use to which the sentence is put implies that the use of *beware* is constrained pragmatically.

Historical explanations provide another relatively common kind of non-syntactic account for ostensibly syntactic phenomena. Historical explanations are legitimate answers to questions like "Why is '2' called *two*?" (It is much easier to write this sensibly than to say it aloud.) Although historical explanations that amount to "It's always been that way as far as the history of the language can be traced" may sometimes obscure the existence of deeper, more explanatory accounts of a different nature (whether syntactic or not), it is clear that at other times it may be futile to hope for a better account. For example, one might imagine that the explanation for the data cited in (1) is not so much a systematic morphological peculiarity as the result of a historical process in which what was originally a phrase *be ware* came to be perceived as a single word, *beware*. If it was a sequence, *be* + *ware*, consisting of a verb and an adjective then naturally forms like **bewore, *bewared, *bewaring* would not be encountered either; if *ware* occurred only after *be* (not after *am*, etc.) it would only occur uninflected because *be* is uninflected, and *ware* is an adjective, and does not inflect. Such an explanation, if correct, would predict the synchronic syntactic facts, although it raises a question for historical syntax: why was *ware* used only after *be*, and not after *is, am, was* or *were*?

Perhaps a simpler example is suggested by the data in (6). It would surely be a futile effort to try to characterize syntactically the sentences that can acceptably consist of just an NP plus an uninflected VP and be used with a single intonation contour to express a wish.

6a. God bless you!
6b. Heaven help us!
6c. *Fred telephone us!
6d. *IBM hire us!

Changes in speech patterns (of whatever source) have preserved as conventional formulae just a fraction of the forms that may once have been generated by fully productive principles. The best one can hope for in a synchronic description is a list of the formulae, as in (7).

7a. God bless/save/damn NP
7b. God/Heaven forbid.
7c. God/Heaven help NP.
    etc.

Another common kind of non-syntactic explanation for apparently syntactic facts is the psychological or processing account. Processing accounts may refer to production (as when it is claimed that certain forms are unacceptable because speakers avoid them because they require too much (mental) effort to produce), or perception (as when it is claimed that certain forms are unacceptable because speakers avoid them because they know (or feel or fear) that hearers will find them too difficult to parse). Properly, probably at least the perceptual explanations are really pragmatic, and not psychological at all, as they appear to involve reasoning. Ross' output constraint on post-verbal constituents (3.41),[3] which stated that constituents which followed the verb optimally occurred in a certain order, would, however, be a syntactic description of the phenomena, since the relevant constructions are characterized in terms of the order of constituents of particular syntactic types. Someone might suggest an alternative, processing description which said something like: "when more than one constituent follows the verb, the constituents that are shortest (or have the least semantic content, or something of the sort) go closest to the verb, because short (or "empty") constituents are hard to stress properly if they go after long ("full") ones." But an account that claimed that short or empty NPs go before long or full ones because the hearer might not notice them or connect them to the verb if they went later would be both a pragmatic and a (folk-)psychological explanation.

Perhaps the most familiar kind of processing explanation for apparently syntactic facts is that offered by Chomsky in *Aspects* for the unacceptability of center embeddings as in (8).

8. That that that Stacy likes you surprises me bothers Tracy irritates Cory.

Such sentences are unacceptable, Chomsky claimed (1965:10–15), not because they are ungrammatical (they could be perfectly grammatical), but because human language processing faculties cannot deal with them (that is, because they are too hard to keep track of).

These are not the only sorts of psychological explanation for distributional facts that can be imagined. Most of the transderivational constraints that have been proposed are pragmatic psychological explanations in syntactic sheep's clothing. For example, a constraint on the distribution of pronouns was proposed which said that pronouns were unacceptable if there were two distinct potential antecedents, as in sentences like (9).

9. John and Bill walked in and he hung up his coat.

Such a constraint would be transderivational in a transformational theory[4] to the extent that it refers to the possibility of two different deep structures (or logical forms), and thus to two different derivations; the resulting sentence is unacceptable in each derivation because of the existence of the other derivation. But a case can be made that the unacceptability of (9) is not a syntactic fact at all, but a pragmatico-psychological one: example (9) is unacceptable,

---

[3] See Chapter 6, Section 2.

[4] And pragmatic in a monostratal theory, to the extent that it refers to potential interpretations which are defined with reference to pragmatic principles.

it may be claimed, because it is impossible for a language user to tell what the intended antecedent of the pronoun is. There is a problem, however, with this sort of explanation (in whatever guise), and that is that it implies that vague and ambiguous sentences like (10) and (11) are unacceptable, and clearly they are not.[5]

10. Mo fixed the TV set by whacking it.

11. Joe Namath had a lot of fans.

Despite the fact that (10) is ambiguous or vague about whether Mo fixed the TV that way by plan or by luck, and vague about where it was whacked, and how hard, etc., and (11) is ambiguous as to whether it is admirers or air-moving devices that Namath had in abundance, (10) and (11) are fully acceptable. Since many fully acceptable sentences are clearly ambiguous, being ambiguous cannot be the basis for a sentence being unacceptable.

An entirely parallel case involves extraposition of relative clauses, as in (12).

12a. A man who says the sky is falling came in.
12b. A man came in who says the sky is falling.

Relative clauses, it has been claimed, cannot be extraposed if the resultant sentence is one that could have been generated independently without extraposition, as shown by the fact that while (12a,b) are interpreted as both making the same claim, (13a) is not understood as saying the same thing as (13b).

13a. Someone who designs computers introduced Minsky to my brother.
13b. Someone introduced Minsky to my brother(,) who designs computers.

The problems with a psychologically-based account of the phenomena illustrated in (9) and (13) are the same: it predicts that ambiguous sentences generally will be unacceptable, and as the acceptability of (10–11) shows, this is not true.

Logical or semantic explanations for (ostensibly) syntactic distributions are also possible, at a variety of levels. Observations of ambiguity, for example, may require either direct semantic explanations (as in cases of lexical

---

[5]It can also be claimed that sentences like (9) are not even categorically unacceptable—that in some circumstances their intended meaning is clear and their use is fully acceptable. If this is so, both processing and syntactic explanations are inappropriate, as the sentence must be considered grammatical, and a (pragmatic) explanation of its (conditional) unacceptability should be sought which refers to the speaker's estimation of the addressee's ability to correctly infer the intended referent.

ambiguity such as (11)), or semantic explanations that are mediated by a syntactic analysis in such a way as to require no special apparatus in either the syntax or the semantics, as is presumably the case with sentences like (14).

14a. Flying planes can be dangerous.

(Planes that fly vs. Piloting planes)

14b. The chickens are ready to eat.

(Chickens which are hungry vs. chickens that will be eaten)

14c. *Zest* makes you feel cleaner than soap.

(...than soap feels vs. ..than soap makes you feel)

Explaining the multiplicity of understandings of a sentence may in other cases, such as the sentences in (15), require a semantic account mediated by pragmatics, or a pragmatic account mediated by semantics.

15a. John may play the tuba.

(It isn't known vs. He is given permission)

15b. Scott is the author of *Waverly*.

(Scott wrote the book vs. Scott and the author are the same person)

15c. Oedipus wanted to marry his mother.

(Oedipus had a desire for incest vs. the woman Oedipus wanted to marry turned out to be his mother)

It should not be assumed that these last ambiguities are well understood, or that there is a single generally accepted theory of their analysis, but most accounts of them that depend on different syntactic structures that have been proposed have been rejected as insufficiently motivated. However, for many kinds of ambiguity it is not at all clear whether a purely semantic or a semantico-pragmatic account is appropriate, or whether a semantic account which follows as a consequence of some structural, syntactic difference is better. Sentence (16) is an example of this sort.

16. Advances in medical technology have made it possible to bring to life people who were considered dead only a few years ago.

(resuscitation vs. resurrection)

Semantic or logical explanations are also offered for the unacceptability of sentences. Such explanations include, for instance, any claim that a sentence's unacceptability is due to logical properties of its meaning, for example, its being a tautology or a contradiction, as in (17–18):

17. The child who threw sand threw sand.

18a. None of the linguists like tofu but some of the linguists do.

18b. I'm taller than I am.

Instead of claiming that a sentence was unacceptable because it violated strict subcategorization principles–a syntactic account–one might claim its unacceptability was a function of its semantics. For example, one might claim that *elapse* represents an intransitive predicate and the semantic component does not provide an interpretation for a direct object NP. Thus, it could be claimed that (19) is unacceptable because the grammar does not provide a semantic interpretation for it.

19. Six months elapsed Morton.

A somewhat similar case involves Perlmutter's (1971) like-subject constraint on deep structures containing verbs like *try*. This was a syntactic account, which claimed that in deep structures with such verbs and sentential complements, the subject of the matrix verb and the subject of the complement had to be identical. One might try to replace it with a logico-semantic (or a pragmatic) account that attributed the unacceptability of sentences like (20) to the fact that *try* represents a relation which holds between an individual and an action by that individual, so that predicating it of an individual and an action by some other individual is nonsense.

20. *Evelyn tried (for) Hilary to play the piano.

Two final kinds of non-syntactic explanations for observations of distributions may be mentioned here, although neither is very commonly justifiable. One refers to phonological properties of the construction in question. For instance, one might suppose, given no other data to start out with, that if sentence (5b) is unacceptable, the reason is that the sequence [bi#bi], where [#] represents a word-boundary, is displeasing to English ears.[6]

5b. You ought to be bewaring of the dog.

This kind of explanation would be a phonological explanation, and would predict that other [bi#bi] sequences would be equally unacceptable. This means that one would expect speakers to reject such sentences as (21):

21a. I will be between planes then.

21b. Her name must be Beatrice.

---

[6]More plausible examples have been proposed (e.g., Ross 1972b, Berman 1974b), but their complexity and syntactic limitations make this hypothetical example a clearer illustration of the nature of the claims at issue.

21c. Where could that bee be?

Phonological explanations for syntactic distributions are not common, but neither are they unheard of. Pullum and Zwicky (1984) discuss a number of issues raised by such interactions of phonology and syntax.

Finally, sentences that appear to be grammatically well-formed may be judged unacceptable by speakers because the ideas they express (in accordance with the normal rules of the language) turn out to be repugnant to speakers asked to judge them. For lack of a better term we may refer to such accounts as cultural descriptions or explanation. A simple and naive example is represented by sentences like (22), which speakers may judge unacceptable, if they do not imagine that falsity is excluded as a cause of unacceptability.

22. The earth is flat, and if you sail too far, you'll fall off the edge.

A more complex and less clear example involves what are known as empathy phenomena in languages like Japanese. In Japanese, the use of a certain verb meaning 'give' *(kureru)* is considered acceptable when the speaker identifies with the recipient more than with the giver, while other verbs meaning 'give' (*yaru* and *ageru*) are considered appropriate if the speaker identifies with the giver more than with the recipient. Since Japanese speakers are expected to identify more with family members than with strangers, sentence (23), where *kuremashita* reflects identification with the recipient referent of the indirect object (the speaker's father) is considered more acceptable than (24), where *agemashita* presupposes identification with the giver referent of the subject, rather than with the recipient.

23. Sono otoko wa   chichi ni   hon o   kuremashita.
    that   man   TOP my-father DAT book ACC gave
    That man gave my father a book.

24. Sono otoko wa   chichi ni   hon o   agemashita.

Discussions of this phenomenon sometimes include claims such as those in (25).

25a. It is easiest for the speaker to empathize with himself; it is next easiest for him to empathize with the hearer; it is more difficult for him to express more empathy with third persons than with either himself or the hearer.

25b. Sentences of such-and-such a description are ruled out because they show arrogance on the part of the speaker (or the subject).

But it is too often not made clear whether the sentences that are rejected as unacceptable are just considered so socially unacceptable (imputing socially unacceptable attitudes to the speaker or individuals mentioned) that speakers cannot bring themselves to acknowledge their grammatical correctness, or whether in fact there is just no conceivable situation that they would be appropriate to represent. (What if someone really did empathize more with his friend than with his father? What if the person really was arrogant and presumptuous?) If there is no situation in which sentences of the sort at issue could be used to accurately report events, then a case could be made that the principles that exclude them are syntactic principles. Otherwise, it seems clear we are dealing with something much more akin to cultural taboos regarding language use, like prohibitions against the use of vulgar words, or words that sound like a dead king's name, than to rules of syntax. Such cultural taboos represent a subspecies of pragmatic explanation that we have chosen to single out with the term cultural. Alternatively, statements like (25a) might be interpreted as representing psychological claims about participants in Japanese culture. In either case, they are pretty clearly not claims about the syntax of the Japanese language.

3 ARGUMENTATION

This chapter characterizes the context and the nature of the discourse that constitutes linguistic argumentation. The first section outlines the assumptions governing linguists' inquiry into both the principles of language and the details of the grammars of particular languages. Subsequent sections describe the ground rules for conducting that research (Sections 2–5) and offer some practical advice on the construction of arguments (Sections 6–8).

3.1 The Role and Nature of Argumentation in Linguistics: Evaluating Claims through Hypothetico-Deductive Inquiry

Linguistics is an empirical science, like biology or physics or astronomy. As such, its goal is the construction of explanatory hypotheses: empirically vulnerable accounts (theories) of observed phenomena. What are the principles governing the formation of sentences in a language, and why do the grammars of languages involve just the kinds of principles they appear to involve, and not other a priori imaginable kinds? Most work in linguistics uses the method of inquiry of hypothetico-deductive argumentation (see the discussion of Popper (1968) in Section 3 below): hypotheses are formulated, predictions are deduced from those hypotheses, the accuracy of those predictions is tested against observation, and hypotheses are deduced to be wrong just in case predictions from them turn out to be inconsistent with observations. Most linguistic argumentation is based on this logic.

In practice, the best hypothesis is deemed to be the simplest one with no empirical failures.[1] Of course, things are rarely so straightforward. Most often,

---

[1] Theoretical considerations ("explanatory adequacy," for example) may also play a role in the choice, perhaps even leading to the choice of a hypothesis with empirical failures, on the grounds that it does a better job of achieving the explanatory goals of the research. When empirical and theoretical factors point in opposite directions (for example, when hypothesis A does a better job than hypothesis B of accounting for the facts under consideration, but B is preferable to A on theoretical grounds), choosing the best hypothesis is a difficult matter, sometimes more like a matter of religion than of science (cf. Kuhn 1970), and good linguists can disagree in ways that are impossible to resolve in a rational way.

no available hypothesis is consistent with all observations, and researchers choose to provisionally accept a hypothesis which makes fewer false predictions than other tested candidates, while they continue the search for an alternative which makes no apparent false predictions. The reason they do not just abandon a falsified hypothesis is that often they need to make assumptions about a certain phenomenon in its domain in order to test hypotheses about some other phenomenon which interacts with it.

It is important to note that within the logic of this form of inquiry, if some[2] of the predictions of a hypothesis are tested, and not found to be false, no conclusion can be deduced about the validity of the hypothesis except that it might be true. This is hardly any help at all, since if it might be true, it might equally well (however much one might doubt it) be false. If you hypothesize that all swans are white, and the next three swans you encounter are in fact white, you still don't know any more than before. The next one you see might still be black. It is in principle impossible, then, to prove any affirmative hypothesis about an interesting, infinite class of phenomena. It is only possible to disprove such a hypothesis, to show that it cannot be correct because it makes incorrect predictions. Strictly speaking, even this is impossible. Strictly speaking, all one can show is that IF certain assumptions are made (e.g., about the extensions (or meanings) of the terms in which the hypothesis is stated), and the predictions of the hypothesis are false, THEN either the hypothesis or one or more of the assumptions is incorrect. It follows that the strength of a conclusion is a direct function of the strength of the assumptions it requires. The message to the analyst is clear: Do not make assumptions lightly, and make critical assumptions explicit.

Thus, a single observation contradicting a single prediction of a hypothesis is sufficient to challenge the hypothesis, indeed, to refute it as stated (or to reject either it or one of the assumptions that warranted deriving the falsified prediction from it), providing, of course, that it is a genuine counterexample— a member of the class about which the claim is made, and its failure to have the property which the hypothesis attributes to it is not the result of some extraordinary accident or some more general, overriding principle. But this cannot be known in advance. The fact that a single genuine counterexample can falsify a hypothesis is the reason that frequency distributions and tests of statistical significance are often not germane to linguistic argumentation. It is irrelevant how many instances falsify a prediction of a hypothesis; one is sufficient to show that it must in some respect be wrong—a thousand of the same type would not show it any more convincingly. On the other hand,

---

[2]Unless the hypothesis concerns a finite class of cases, it makes an infinite number of predictions, and it is in principle impossible to test the validity of all of its predictions.

if three instances of different types indicate that the hypothesis (and/or its underpinnings) is wrong in three different respects, then this is a stronger indication of defects in the hypothesis.

For ease of exposition, the illustrative examples in this chapter are largely hypothetical or very circumscribed. It might have been instructive to use genuine arguments cited or presupposed in the linguistic literature of the past 30 years as examples, but given what is involved in building a sound argument, as described in Sections 1–5, any convincing real example would have to be embedded in several pages of justifications of assumptions, and the points to be illustrated would likely get lost in the supporting exposition.

The fact that many of the examples relate directly to the distribution of natural language expressions should not be taken to imply that syntactic research is concerned exclusively with the detailed grammatical description of particular languages, or that only such research is governed by the principles described here. It should be evident from Chapter 2 that much research in syntax begins with hypotheses that are consequences of fairly high-level theoretical principles. The investigation of such hypotheses is governed by the same logic and values as govern the investigation of the empirical questions that they must inevitably boil down to. The principles of argumentation and presentation described here and in Chapter 4 are not specific to any particular kind of question, to any particular denomination of syntactic theory, indeed, not specific to syntax or even to linguistics. They should serve the reader well in any situation where rational persuasion is called for.

3.2 The Empiricalness of Linguistic Argumentation

The logic of hypothetico-deductive inquiry also requires that the hypothesis being investigated be **intersubjectively testable** (cf. Popper 1968), which means simply that it can be tested by other investigators and be expected to derive the same empirical results. It is equivalent to the requirement of reproducibility of results which is familiar from research in the physical and behavioral sciences. The consequence of this requirement for doing argumentation (and analysis too, for that matter, since analysis involves tacit internal argumentation) is that hypotheses must be framed (and phrased) so that they do not require subjective interpretation–indeed, so that they leave no room for subjective interpretation–of what they really (are intended to) say. This means that a hypothesis must be precise, and not vague in any respect (on which, more below), and must not depend on any undefined terms. The requirement of precision is really a consequence of intersubjective testability, although that is not always immediately obvious. To see how the requirement of intersubjective testability precludes adopting vague hypotheses, let us consider hypothesis A, which is shot through with vagueness.

A. The topic is the first constituent in the sentence.

To test this hypothesis, we need to know:

a) how to identify topics independently of this claim about their distribution,

b) what is meant by *sentence*,

c) how to identify the first constituent in a sentence.

If Hypothesis A is not supplemented with a definition of *topic*, we either cannot test it at all, because we will be unable to identify topics in order to determine whether they are in fact the first constituent in their respective sentences; or, at the very least, we cannot expect that what we might interpret *topic* to have been intended (by the framer of the hypothesis) to refer to is what it actually was intended to refer to. Suppose that Hypothesis A is supplemented with a definition of *topic*, namely (B):

B. The topic of a sentence is, by definition, the phrase that refers to what the sentence is about.

We are not much better off. We still do not know what *sentence* is intended to refer to—does it refer to material dominated by any S-node in a conventional representation, material dominated by the highest S-node in such a representation, to the utterance of something which in conventional orthography begins with a capital letter and ends with a period, or what? Even if what is meant by *sentence* is specified more clearly, nothing guarantees that judgements by different investigators of what a given sentence is "about" will be the same. Because *about* is a vague term, whose interpretation may depend on interpretations of the context in which it is used, we can expect contradictory judgements of what the topic of a sentence like (1) is.

1. Kim wrote a letter to Sandy.

Judgements might indicate any of the following as the topic: 'Kim', 'Sandy', 'writing', 'writing a letter', 'Kim writing a letter to Sandy'.

Finally, supposing that it were possible to identify topics and sentences uniquely and uniformly across analysts, we still could not expect uniform judgements as to whether particular topic identifications for certain individual sentences corroborated or disconfirmed hypothesis A, because it is not clear what to count as the first constituent of a sentence. For example, in the following sentence, it is unclear what criteria would dictate counting *a*, *a man*, or *a man who has three ears* as the first constituent.

2. A man who has three ears just came in.

Because even such an apparently straightforward designation as *the first constituent* is insufficient to uniquely designate a referent in a particular domain (such as sentence (2)), analysts interpreting it differently may come to contradictory conclusions regarding the proposition that Hypothesis A makes false predictions about sentence (2).

3.3 Precision

The scenario just presented illustrates the importance of precision in formulating hypotheses. The more precise a hypothesis, the more empirical (i.e., testable) it is, and the easier to test (cf. Popper 1968). It is because they value precision, for these reasons, that linguists sometimes seem to be preoccupied with formidable-looking formal representations of their analyses. The primary purpose of a formalism, beyond the requirement for explicitness that it enforces, is to provide a way to formulate hypotheses that makes it possible to use techniques of formal (deductive) logic to derive predictions; a completely formalized system of representation precludes the expression of vague or imprecise claims. The statements it allows can be depended on to be precise and therefore intersubjectively testable. It is usually relatively easy to see if they make incorrect predictions (usually they do on the analyst's first try), and if so, where the problem is. Working within a formal system also discourages inconsistency; as long as the formalism is consistent, inconsistent analyses are that much more conspicuous when one attempts to represent them formally. Thus, it is important not to confuse complicated graphs and diagrams and funny-looking symbols with formalization. A system is a formal system only if (like first-order predicate calculus, for example) there are explicit rules defining what statements are (formally, i.e., syntactically) well-formed, explicit rules defining how each of the well-formed statements is to be interpreted, and explicit rules of inference for deriving logical consequences from sets of statements.

There is another advantage to formalization, and that is that the mathematical properties of formalisms are relatively well-understood. If an analysis is represented in terms of such a formalism, predictions about the phenomenon analyzed can be made from properties of the formal system. These often concern properties of the phenomenon which might otherwise go unnoticed. Of course, the advantages of formalism are necessary properties only of fully formalized systems; an incomplete formalism can be worse than no formalism at all.[3] There is no magic in mathematical notations; if used with precision, ordinary language is a pretty dependable workhorse.[4]

In any case, being precise, whether in English, or some more formal language, not only provides higher empirical content, it also ensures that a claim does not say more than its author intends it to. To see this, suppose that a linguist makes the following observation:

> "When speakers judge (3) to be unacceptable, they assume that *he* and *John* must be intended to refer to the same individual.
>
> 3. He thinks John is stupid.
>
> Speakers who judge (3) to be acceptable assume that *he* and *John* are intended to refer to distinct individuals."

The linguist might express this observation as any one of the following claims.

C. Judgements of the acceptability of (3) depend on the informant's beliefs about the world.

D. Judgements of the acceptability of (3) depend on the informant's beliefs about whether the speaker intended *he* and *John* to refer to the same individual.

E. Speakers judge (3) to be acceptable unless they assume that *he* and *John* are intended to refer to the same individual.

All of these claims are consistent with the generalization the linguist intends, but only (E) states that generalization precisely. Claim (C) in its vagueness is also consistent with the hypothesis that judgements of acceptability on (3) depend on whether the informant believes in Santa Claus or supply-side economics. Claim (D) is narrow enough to rule out such possibilities, but still does not state the dependence explicitly, while (E) does: (D) would also be consistent with the claim that speakers who believed *he* and *John* to be coreferential would be the ones who judge (3) to be acceptable.

Sometimes people think that being vague will cover up uncertainty on their part, and it may, up to a point. But on close inspection, rather than covering up holes or flaws, vagueness draws attention to them, like a bandage draws

---

[3] See Borkin et al. (1971, Section 1) for description of some of the inadequacies of the incomplete formalism that was conventional for describing Standard Theory transformational rules.

[4] Compare the accuracy and precision of the formal descriptions of transformational rules in introductory texts to that of the ordinary language formulations that their authors provide ubiquitously (and cast aspersions on), e.g., Akmajian and Heny 1975, Chapter 5.

attention to a wound. Occasionally a writer will carry explicitness too far, but excessive explicitness is much easier to amend than vagueness. There is no risk of writing a faulty argument from being over-explicit, but the linguist who indulges in vague claims runs a great risk of advancing an argument with faulty premises, or one whose conclusions do not follow from its premises.

3.4 Universality

We have emphasized the importance of stating a hypothesis precisely; if it is not stated precisely, it cannot be tested, for it will not be possible to determine exactly what predictions it makes. But it is not enough for a hypothesis to be precise; a hypothesis can be perfectly precise and be of very little value if its predictions do not extend beyond a finite domain. A universal hypothesis has a universal quantifier (e.g., *all, never*) or equivalent (*if*), and therefore makes a claim about every element in an indefinitely large domain. To qualify as explanatory, a hypothesis must cover as large a domain as possible, so that observations about particular cases are treated as automatic consequences following from a more general principle.

For instance, as it stands, (E) is precise enough to test, and may stand a good chance of being corroborated, but it is not very general. Indeed, it makes predictions about only one sentence, namely, (3). Could it follow as an automatic consequence of some more nearly universal hypothesis such as (F), (G), (H), or (I)?

F. The pronoun *he* can never precede its antecedent[5] if *he* is the subject of a verb and the antecedent is the subject of a clause which is the object of that verb.

G. A pronoun can never precede its antecedent when the pronoun is the subject of a verb and the antecedent is part of the object complement of that verb.

H. A pronoun can never precede its antecedent if the antecedent is in a subordinate clause relative to the pronoun.

I. Pronouns can never precede their antecedents.

In fact, (E) follows from each of the claims (F-I). The problem is to determine which one is the most general one that is consistent with the facts. The task of the linguist is to find the strongest, most general way of stating the claim. A good rule of thumb might be to formulate the strongest claim that you think might be supportable, and then extend it to a more nearly universal domain, as

---

[5]Where *antecedent* of a pronoun is defined as "a phrase understood as having the same intended referent as that pronoun."

(F) extends (E), and (G) extends (F), and so on. In other words, make a bolder claim, and try to support that. This is a recursive procedure: if the stronger claim is corroborated, one should extend it some more, and see if it is still supportable.

In general, a conscientious researcher will always try to see if the claim at issue can be deduced from a claim with a higher order of universality. This means that whenever you are satisfied that you have explained some phenomenon, or part thereof, however large or small, you step back and ask yourself: why should that be the explanation? Why shouldn't the opposite be the case? What general principle could it be a consequence of? In practice, you would always have to stop somewhere, but trying to answer such questions is a direct way of discovering the limits of a theory.

It goes without saying that it is necessary to test every piece of your claim. For instance, asked to state the distribution of present tense used for future time reference, as in (4-5), one might, on examination of a much larger data set, come up with claim (J).

  4. Kim leaves tomorrow.
  5. *It rains tomorrow.

  J. The present tense can be used in finite clauses referring to future time provided that the event described in the clause is presumed to be pre-arranged, and there is some adverbial expression in the clause which specifies the time reference as being in the future.

It is not enough to argue for this claim by saying that it correctly predicts that (4) is acceptable and (5) is not. One must address individually the issues of prearrangement and adverbial time expressions, and argue, for instance, that a sentence like (6) will be considered acceptable if it is assumed that Brutus' death could have been scheduled (and not merely predicted), but unacceptable if it is assumed that it could not possibly have been prearranged.

  6. Brutus dies tomorrow.

Likewise, it is necessary to show that the presence of an adverbial referring to future time is required in addition, for the sentences to be acceptable. This means presenting acceptable sentences with the correct kind of expression, paired with unacceptable sentences that are identical except that the expression is absent (**negative evidence**), and further, showing that sentences with adverbial expressions that do not specify future time fail in the same way as sentences with no adverbial. And so on.

3.5   The Danger of Ad Hoc Hypotheses

There is a temptation, when trying to find a plausible hypothesis which will serve the twin masters of Precision and Universality without being obviously false, to succumb to the lure of ad hoc hypotheses.[6] When a promising hypothesis is corroborated to some degree and confronted with a class of counterexamples, it is very tempting to revise the hypothesis so that it excludes those cases by mere fiat. If your pet hypothesis Q says that all Xs have property Y, and you discover that Xs that are also As do not have property Y, it is a natural reaction to alter your hypothesis to Q': "All Xs that are not As have property Y." Now your hypothesis (Q') is less universal, and thus has a lower empirical content. It is no longer falsified by the class of counterexamples that falsified Q, but only because it has been artificially protected against falsification by the ad hoc restriction. Only when you can corroborate some other more general hypothesis, like "Items of kind A never have property Y," from which it follows that Xs that are As will not have property Y, will the ad hoc modification to Q cease to be ad hoc, and be a motivated (justified) restriction.

Ad hoc hypotheses (equivalently: ad hoc restrictions on hypotheses) are an embarrassment to a theory because they reduce its empirical content by making it less vulnerable to falsification, and betray a greater affection for the theory than for an explanatory account of the facts. Popper (1968) contains extensive discussion of this point, and Zwicky (1973) presents a detailed example from English syntax.

3.6   Kinds of Arguments

Several kinds of arguments are common in syntactic research, for example: arguments that a certain sequence of categories does or does not form a constituent, arguments that an expression does or does not belong to some grammatical category, arguments that sentences of a certain form are generated by some particular rule, arguments that sentences of a certain sort have a representation with a certain property, arguments that one hypothesis about the representation of sentences of a certain sort is better than another hypothesis. They are all, however, reducible to a single type—the comparison of hypotheses. This is not always obvious: arguments that *there* is inserted by a transformational rule in the derivation of sentences like (7) do not appear to involve a comparison of hypotheses.

7.   There is a City Council meeting tonight.

---

[6]Popper (1968) refers to these as "auxiliary hypotheses."

But implicitly, they do; they contrast the predictions made by the hypothesis that *there* is inserted by a transformational rule with the hypothesis that *there* is not present as the result of a transformational rule, but is base-generated (i.e., generated directly by phrase structure rules) in its surface structure position—a null hypothesis. Commentary like "If *there* were not inserted transformationally, we would expect ..." may be the only clue to the comparative nature of the argument.

Similarly, the category membership arguments like that in (8) work by comparing the hypothesis (M) that a certain phrase belongs to some particular category to the hypothesis (M′) that that phrase does not belong to that category, and finding the latter inferior on the grounds that it unnecessarily complicates the description of the language since it would depend on the claim that the generalization in assumption (K) was incorrect and must be replaced by the disjunction (K′).

8. K. Anything that has certain properties belongs to this category.
   L. That phrase has these properties.
   Therefore:
   M. That phrase is a member of this category.

K′. Anything with certain properties belongs to this category or is that phrase.

All things being equal, entities in a theory should not be multiplied unnecessarily.[7] This warrants rejection of (K′) if, all other things being equal, (K) and (L) are correct.

Likewise, the arguments that sequences of formatives with the analysis X-Y-Z form a constituent are implicitly comparisons of the predictions of that hypothesis with the predictions of the hypothesis that they do not form a single constituent.

Hypotheses may be compared on either empirical or logical (explanatory) grounds. Hypothesis A may be preferred to Hypothesis B because B predicts that certain acceptable sentences are ungrammatical, while A predicts they are grammatical. If A and B make the same predictions about the grammaticality of relevant types of sentences, B may still be preferred to A on the grounds that B is a more general hypothesis (see Section 4): its predictions follow from general principles needed in the grammar independently of the phenomenon at issue, while Hypothesis A entails ad hoc rules or conditions whose only function is to keep Hypothesis A from being empirically inadequate.

---

[7]This principle is known as Ockham's Razor (or Occam's Razor) after William of Ockham.

3.7 The Form of Arguments

As must be evident by now, an argument is a demonstration that a claim (the conclusion of the argument) makes certain predictions, given certain particular assumptions about the properties of the entities it refers to; that these predictions are borne out by observations about the phenomenon (the evidence for the conclusion); and that an opposing claim makes contrary predictions which are in fact refuted by that evidence. The simplest arguments have the following components or logical structure:

[Claim]
Instances of expressions of type C are acceptable if and only if conditions X, Y, and Z are met.

[Predictions]
This predicts that sentences containing expressions of type C will be acceptable when conditions X, Y, and Z are met, but unacceptable if any one or more of them is not met.

[Evidence]
These predictions are borne out. Sentences (a–c), where X, Y, and Z all obtain, are acceptable.
[sentences a–c]
However, examples (d–e), where X does not hold because [cited expression(s)] has property A rather than property X, are unacceptable.
[sentences d–e]
Similarly, examples (f–g), where Y does not hold because [cited expression(s)] has property B rather than property Y, are unacceptable.
[sentences f–g]
Likewise, examples (h–i), where Z does not hold because [cited expression] has property D rather than property Z, are unacceptable.
[sentences h–i]

[Conclusion]
Thus, expressions of type C are acceptable only if conditions Z, Y, and Z are satisfied.

The present tense for future time argument described above will have essentially this structure. As demonstrated in Ch. 4, it is more effective to present data corroborating the individual predictions one by one than all at once.

The claim in such arguments is being implicitly compared to a null hypothesis: the claim that expressions of type C occur freely—regardless of whether conditions X, Y, and Z are met. The null hypothesis is refuted if examples with such expressions where X, Y, and Z are not met are in fact unacceptable, for this shows that these expressions do not occur freely.

Arguments this simple are commonly used in motivating claims that are used as premises in other arguments, for example, in motivating the claim that ordinary reflexive pronouns must have clausemate antecedents in order to argue that a certain structure must be ascribed to some construction containing a reflexive pronoun. If an argument is any more complex than this, it is helpful, to both the writer, and whatever readers there may be, to spell out the opposing hypothesis, and frame the argument explicitly as a comparison of hypotheses. This usually also serves as a prod to make explicit the assumptions that the predictions from the claims depend on, since the more explicitly an argument is expressed, the clearer its dependence on its assumptions becomes. In any case, it is always a good idea to make the assumptions your argument depends on explicit, and if possible, to show what motivates them. If it should turn out that some evidence shows your hypothesis to be better than an opposing hypothesis, while other evidence shows that hypothesis to be better than your hypothesis, there is a good chance that such contradictory conclusions stem from one or more incorrect assumptions; having the assumptions spelled out in black and white (and having their motivations at hand) makes it easier to track down which one (or ones) is incorrect and should be replaced.

Whatever the complexity of the argument, there should be an explanation of how the sentences (and acceptability judgements on them) that constitute the data provide the evidence that you say they do. It is not enough to just say that they show that the claim makes (in)correct predictions; you have to show how it indicates that the predictions are (in)correct. In addition, not only is it necessary to show that the relevant facts follow from your claim, and are not merely consistent with it, it is also necessary to show that they conflict with the predictions made by alternative theories or claims.

3.8   Troubleshooting

"Argument, shmargument! I can't even figure out what I want to claim!"

If you can only come up with a list of observations, when trying to describe some phenomenon, you are probably missing a generalization. Try to figure out what would predict at least some of the observations; if you can do that, you can restate it as a generalization from which those observations will follow as consequences, and proceed to test it.

"I know what I want to claim, but I don't know how to say why I think it's right."

It often helps to ask: what would be the consequences for the description of these facts of making the opposite claim? How does making your claim improve the situation? When you have this figured out, you have the basis for a straightforward comparison of hypotheses argument.

"I'm sure my argument is logical, but I can't figure out how to explain the logic of it."

It is necessary to distinguish clearly among:

1) your claim (your answer to the question at issue),
2) the assumptions it rests on (definitions of terms, the set of possible alternatives allowed within the theory),
3) the predictions you derive from it (stated in general terms, not in terms of specific sentences),
4) additional assumptions you have relied on to derive those predictions (e.g., claims about phenomena (like passive structures or reflexive forms) that are used to examine differences between two theories).

When you can do this, your argument will just about put itself together, and wear its logic on its sleeve.

"Comments on my work say that I've left out a step, that I've left a crucial assumption unstated, but my argument looks complete and straightforward to me. How can I find the assumption that's supposed to be missing?"

Usually when an assumption or premise is left out, it is because it is an assumption that seems to the writer perfectly obvious and unchallengeable— so obvious that it's part of the furniture, so to speak. If it is obvious to the reader also, the argument will not seem incoherent, but it may not be obvious to the reader, and it may not be unchallengeable; it might be false. Because of this possibility, it is always safer to err on the side of overexplaining.

Sometimes translating an argument into arbitrary symbols helps to flush out the missing premise. For example, argument (N) can be abstracted as (N').

N. The sequence *that S* is an NP because it occurs in subject position.

N'. Expressions of type X belong to category Y because they have property P.

From examination of (N'), it is immediately clear that it does not follow that X is a member of category Y unless the assumption is made that only members of category Y have property P—this is the missing premise. This means that argument (N') is properly (re)constructed as (N''').

N''. Premise: If an element has property P, it belongs to category Y.
Observation: Expressions of type X have property P.
Conclusion: Expressions of type X belong to category Y.

Note that the premise of (N'') does not entail that every member of Y has property P. Consequently, observing that some members of that category do not have this property does not invalidate the premise.

By simply translating these arbitrary symbols back into the meaningful phrases they replaced, we can reconstruct (N) as a complete argument, as in (N''').

N'''. Premise: If an element can occur in subject position, it is an NP.
Observation: The sequence *that S* occurs in subject position, as
                shown by the fact that ....
Conclusion: The sequence *That S* is an NP.

The fact that one is able to make explicit the assumption on which an argument depends does not, of course, make it a valid assumption, but it is a lot easier to evaluate its validity, and the validity of the argument it supports, when it is explicitly stated.

Another example. The argument (O) can be translated into symbols as (O').

O. Imperatives allow tags with the pronoun *you*, so they must have an underlying subject *you*.

O'. Construction A has property B, so it has property C also.

It is obvious that O' is not a valid argument as it stands. It is missing a premise, namely that all constructions with property B have property C also. When that premise is stated explicitly, the argument appears as (O''), and from (O'') it is easy to reconstruct (O) as a complete argument, as in (O''').

O″. Premise:　　All constructions with property B have property C also.
　　Observation: Construction A has property B.
　　Conclusion: Construction A has property C.

O‴.Premise:　　All sentences with tags have subjects which agree with those tags in person, number and gender.
　　Observation: Imperatives have 2nd person tags.
　　Conclusion: Imperatives have 2nd person subjects.

One last caution. If you read much of the older (1960s) literature in transformational grammar, you will come across arguments (typically arguments that such-and-such a phenomenon is to be accounted for by a transformational rule) that rely on phenomena that produce comparable deviance in the constructions that are claimed to be related by the rule. For example, it used to be argued that the parallelism between the sentences in (9) and the corresponding sentences in (10) represents a generalization that is best expressed if the sentences in (10) are somehow derived from structures underlying those in (9).

9a. A bird is in the garden.
9b. A bird is during the garden.

10a. There is a bird in the garden.
10b. *There is a bird during the garden.

This conclusion is not warranted, as can be seen by examining the structure of the argument, given as (P).

P. Premise:　　X is deviant.
　　Observation: X+Y is deviant in the same way.
　　Conclusion: X and X+Y have the same deep structure, and Y is inserted by an optional transformational rule.

The conclusion does not follow from the premise and the observations without a host of other assumptions, which would not all be assented to. For example, the sequence X+Y would be just as deviant if it were basegenerated, like X. Thus, if some sentential construction is deviant, it will be just as deviant, and in the same way, if you put the word *obviously* in front of it, but this would never have been considered evidence that *obviously* should be generated by an insertion transformation, rather than by phrase-structure rules.

4 PRESENTATION

As we said earlier, presentation is no small problem. A well-done analysis with good solid arguments can be wasted if it is poorly presented. The facts of life are that any research enterprise is also a social enterprise in an important way: the results have to be disseminated in some fashion to the other members of the profession, sometimes even more widely. Dissemination itself is not the goal, of course; the goal is to get your professional colleagues to consider your ideas and hypotheses, take them seriously, and accept them on their merits. This goal can be frustrated, in fact, very likely will be frustrated, if the research is presented in a way that obscures the point of the presentation and the strength of its arguments. It is a good question whether research is worth doing if nobody ever learns about it; but at any rate, most people consider the goal of research to be the advancement of the state of human knowledge, not just the knowledge of the person doing the research. If your work is poorly presented, it is likely to be judged as poor research, or perhaps misinterpreted as saying more or less than you intend to be understood as saying, and is likely not to be appreciated on the merits of its content. As a consequence, it will not be taken seriously, and will not be added to the belief system that makes up the content of the field.

We belabor this point because linguists often fail to appreciate the importance of clear writing, for a variety of reasons. One reason is a common belief that if a person is brilliant, it will somehow come through in writing, even if the writing is haphazard; just to express the ideas in some fashion will dazzle the reader, and the world will swoon at your feet. This is clearly false.

Some linguists underestimate the importance of writing because (they believe) they are already good writers. That is, they have either a gift or an acquired talent for writing that kind of prose that all of us like best to read: sophisticated literary prose, the language of novelists, essayists, and poets. They can move us, entertain us, puzzle us, provide us with all the literary analogues of the rides on the carnival midway. Unfortunately, this is precisely the kind of writing that is most likely to obscure things in a research paper. What is needed for reporting research is transparent, unexciting language that does not overshadow and obscure the research being reported. Some beginning linguists find it difficult at first to rein in their natural verbal exuberance and write in the plainest of plain language. But at least in the beginning austerity is a useful discipline. Some linguists are able to develop an elegant personal style while maintaining extreme clarity, but it usually takes considerable practice at plain writing.

Most writers don't think analytically about the process of writing—they just sit down, organize their thoughts, and start writing. This method works fine for some writers. If writing this way comes easy for you, and you're satisfied with the clarity of your writing, then you needn't read further.

But if you find writing difficult, or if you have trouble achieving the kind of clarity you want, it would be worth your while to think consciously and analytically about the choices you make unconsciously when you write. One of the most important of these choices is the choice of reader. Most of us don't have a specific reader consciously in mind when we write research papers. Some beginning writers write as if they were writing for the most critical, nit-picking kind of reader, which can lead the writer to an overly defensive kind of writing, even to writer's block: how can I possibly write to satisfy this hostile reader? Other beginners appear to write for their advisor or professor, a person to whom they attribute not only superior knowledge of everything that they themselves know, but also phenomenal abilities to infer relations between independent facts. Since they feel it would be impertinent to explain things to such a superior scholar, and their ultimate goal is to make an impression as knowledgeable and insightful, their prose tends to presuppose too much, and their explanations are way too sketchy for mere mortals to understand. Still others write as if they themselves were the intended readers. This leads to a writing style where referents for pronouns and other anaphoric expressions are often impossible for a reader to determine, and explanations are marked by reasoning from unstated assumptions. The consequence is that their prose is nearly impossible for anyone besides themselves to understand. Some writers may even write different sections for different readers, making their writing nearly incoherent.

Most successful writers know that writing clear and effective prose is much easier if you make conscious decisions about the intended reader. Imagine your paper being read by an actual person, or even an imaginary one with the right characteristics. A good strategy for linguistics papers is always to assume that the reader is trained in linguistics, intelligent but not brilliant, with a limited attention span. It's a good idea to let your real or imaginary reader be somebody with an open mind, and just a little familiarity with the topic of your discussion, who will stop you when they can't follow what you are saying or don't understand why you draw the conclusions you draw.

4.1   Organization

The key to clear prose is to be clear in your own mind about what you want to show in the paper, and to tell the reader up front that this is what you are attempting to show. The instant the reader loses track of what you are doing at any point in the paper, the game may be lost. In expository writing, readability is increased considerably by starting out with a clear discussion of what the paper is about, followed by a brief sketch of the organization of the rest of the paper. Rhetoricians have always known this, and psychologists (e.g., Bransford and Johnson 1973) have carried out experiments that show it conclusively. You can demonstrate this fact to yourself by reading the following passage from Bransford and Johnson's experiment.

> The procedure is actually quite simple. First you arrange things into different groups. Of course, one pile may be sufficient depending on how much there is to do. If you have to go somewhere else due to lack of facilities that is the next step, otherwise you are pretty well set. It is important not to overdo things. That is, it is better to do too few things at once than too many. In the short run this may not seem important but complications can easily arise. A mistake can be expensive as well. At first the whole procedure will seem complicated. Soon, however, it will become just another facet of life. It is difficult to foresee any end to the necessity for this task in the immediate future, but then one can never tell. After the procedure is completed one arranges the materials into different groups again. Then they can be put into their appropriate places. Eventually they will be used once more and the whole cycle will then have to be repeated. However, that is part of life.

How well do you understand this paragraph after reading it? Bransford and Johnson found that most readers did not understand it well at all, though of course each sentence is perfectly comprehensible. If you are like most people, the passage will be opaque to you, even though each sentence seems like it ought to make sense. If you really understood the passage, it was because you made a good guess about the (unstated!) point of the passage, and that allowed you to make sense of it. If you now re-read the passage with the extra bit of information that it is entitled "Washing Clothes," it should suddenly be much easier to understand. The moral of this is: say at the beginning what the paper is about, rather than leaving it to the reader to figure out.

In general, you should not expect the reader to understand more than what you state explicitly. The single most common failing in student research papers is a failure to be explicit, which requires the reader to make a special effort to guess what it is the student is trying to say or show. A very common marginal comment on students' papers is "What is the point of this passage? What are you trying to show?" The key, then, is to take pains to make it clear to the reader at every point in the paper what the point of every passage is; to be like a vaudeville magician in first saying, "I will now do such-and-such," and then doing such-and-such. If doing it took more than a page or two, remind the reader that what you have just done is such-and-such. Briefly summarizing your argument in this way before presenting it, and again after presenting it (to leave the readers certain of what they have been persuaded of) has the additional advantage of inviting the analyst to check its validity each time she writes or reads it.

This simple strategy entails various kinds of tactics in writing. First, be clear about exactly what you are trying to do at every point. You may find it useful to make an outline as a means of making clearer to yourself what the structure of your work is. If you find you can't make one, then something is wrong and need to think a while longer, to clarify in your mind what the structure of the paper ought to be (see Chapter 3 for some hints about the structure of arguments).

The noun phrase *the structure of the paper* raises an important point. It makes sense to speak not only of the structure of the arguments, but of texts (in this case, research papers) as well. It is incumbent on the writer to make clear to the reader just what both are. Not just by indicating the relations among parts at transitions from one part to the next, but by previewing them at the outset. Avoid the temptation to spring surprises on the reader. Research papers should not have punchlines. You are aiming to induce the argument within your reader, not to dazzle her with leaps of logic and a surprise conclusion.

You may discover that there can be almost as much pleasure in reading a well-written linguistic argument as there is in reading a Shakespearean tragedy, and perhaps for the same reason: you know what's going to happen, you anticipate the outcome, and appreciate the masterfulness with which the author makes it appear inevitable.

It may be worthwhile to consider a few more things to avoid in presenting your arguments. Do not begin an argument (or a paper) as so many linguists do, by saying, "Consider the following sentences," then listing the sentences. Pay no attention to the fact that some well-known linguists do it; after a while you will begin to find it inconsiderate and annoying. Why? Because you don't know what you're looking for. When presentation of evidence begins that way, it in effect demands that the reader read the sentences twice: first as they appear in the expository order of the paper, then again when you tell him what is important about them; at this point it will be necessary to go back and read them again.[1] It is a much better idea to indicate the significance of the data (example sentences) before you display them, so that the reader can tell what you think is relevant about them. The most effective (and considerate) way to introduce example sentences is to not mention them by number until you have explained just what facts about them are relevant to the task at hand. Once referred to, they should go immediately after the first prose sentence that mentions them. Restricting the placement of examples to immediately after the first sentence that mentions them effectively precludes introducing more than a few examples at a time.

The same strategy applies to the organization of entire arguments. It is much more effective to describe the hypothesis first (or better yet, describe the differences between two contrasting hypotheses), and then spell out the implied claims. At that point it is helpful to outline their predictions, in terms of what sorts of judgements they predict will be made about what classes of sentences. Only then is it useful to present relevant data, saying in very explicit terms how they bear on the claims. Example sentences should never be introduced until their relevance has been made clear in this way. The prose that introduces example sentences needs to say which sentences bear on which claim, and how (or why) their acceptability or unacceptability supports or disconfirms the claim. After you have described how the data refute or corroborate the predictions of the hypotheses, you should say explicitly what conclusion about the hypothesis is to be drawn from the data you have presented. For every argument, you need to say how the data you cite are evidence for what you say they are evidence for. Apparently it is impossible to emphasize this too much. It is never enough to just display the crucial data; you have to characterize them, i.e., say what properties make them crucial for supporting or falsifying a hypothesis. You should not expect the reader to do it.

---

[1] In the same class, under most circumstances, is the so-called "straw man" exposition. This is occasionally a useful device in pedagogical rhetoric, whereby writers pretend to propose a hypothesis they know to be incorrect, only to show why it is inadequate. Doing this well takes talent and a feel for which ultimately incorrect proposals will appear on superficial examination to be obviously correct. In the right hands, this kind of exposition can be very effective. In the wrong hands, it's tiresome. (It is not a form of argument, by the way, but merely a rhetorical device of exposition and staging.) Save it for when you write a textbook.

Explicating your argument this way should clearly delineate the structure of the paper. Around each argument you will have:

(a) a statement of the hypothesis the argument relates to,

(b) an examination of the implied claims to be tested,

(c) a discussion of the nature of the data which are relevant for testing the hypothesis (or deciding between two hypotheses),

(d) a discussion of what the data show about that conclusion, including, for arguments of more than minimal complexity, an explication of just how it is that they show what you say they do.

Given this, your paper would consist of a series of unconnected arguments. Connecting them is a matter of grouping the arguments in related groups, and stating the relations between them. The best strategy, then, at least until you develop a comfortable style of your own, is first to do the analysis to your satisfaction. Then, when you are ready to begin writing,

(1) Consider making an outline of the points you want to make in the paper. Some people find this an indispensable step.

(2) Write a section that describes the problem. This should consist of:

(a) a section that introduces the phenomenon to be analyzed, with some illustrative examples of it.

(b) a presentation[2] of the problem: the hypothesis you want to argue for or against, or of some pair of hypotheses you want to compare empirically, stated as precisely as possible without presupposing familiarity with notions or facts that it is unreasonable to expect. Exact details of the analysis will come later in the presentation.

(c) a discussion of why anybody should care. What you say here depends upon the kind of paper you are writing. If you are presenting an account of some previously unanalyzed phenomenon, there is not much you need to say here. If your work is theoretically oriented, say how your conclusion bears on questions of linguistic theory. If the reason for the analysis is that you need the conclusion as a premise in another argument (i.e., you want to build

---

[2]Be careful about framing your claim in technical jargon. If you have not fully mastered the technical terminology, your decision to use it may obscure the content of your claims to a point where a non-sympathetic reader will not have the faintest idea what you are claiming, or how to go about looking for a counterexample, something he ought to be able to do easily, in principle.

something on it), then say so briefly. And be as explicit here as in the rest of the paper.

(3) Describe the logic of your arguments about the hypotheses: explain, in general terms, why you reached the conclusion you did. This includes a statement of assumed premises (regardless of whether they are axioms (things taken for granted by the theory, but not argued for) or theorems (conclusions whose correctness has been argued), including, if relevant, what general theoretical framework is being assumed. It also includes a discussion of the general nature of the predictions made by the claim in conjunction with its premises, a statement that they are borne out, and an explanation of how the conclusions follow from the premises. End by describing the structure of the rest of the paper; for example, "The first section demonstrates [...], then in section 2, [...] will be examined. In the third section I argue on the basis of these facts, that [...]" etc. Be specific enough for the reader to grasp what the paper is about and how it is organized.

(4) Lay out the heart of the paper: the arguments. At this point, present the specific hypothesis or hypotheses to be examined, then the arguments for them, structured and presented in the way discussed above. If this section is very long, make sure it has signposts for the reader. For example, if you go through a very long and involved argument, summarize it briefly at the end, especially if the next section depends on the conclusion of this argument. When you begin each argument, describe at the beginning what the structure of the argument is, just as you did with the paper as a whole. for example, "I will argue in this section that..., by showing that such-and-such." This gets easier with practice. Always keep in mind that the reader will be easily distracted from your point. You can assume that your reader is reasonably knowledgeable about linguistics, but is not as intensely interested in your topic as you are, and so may tend to forget things, and nod off now and then.

(5) At the end of your chain of arguments, provide a summary and a restatement of the general conclusion of your paper, perhaps with a little more discussion of its implications, if relevant.

As a consequence of this strategy, your paper will be clearly structured, with repeated instances of the same kind of structure: you announce what you are going to do, then do it, then summarize and discuss. It may also involve embedded occurrences of this same kind of structure. Thus, a perspicuously written paper (or section) has the following structure:

I. Claim: the "bottom line"—the conclusion of your analysis, stated as precisely as possible. Try for under 50 words.

II. Summary of the logic of the argument for the claim.

III. Specific predictions of the claim in the context of the relevant assumptions, paired with evidence (observations, data) showing that the predictions are borne out. Remember that particular example sentences are not evidence in and of themselves. Your predictions are about judgements regarding the acceptability of particular sentences; your evidence will be judgements concerning exemplars of those sentences.

IV. Summary of the argument. Describe the consequences of the evidence taken together with the assumptions. Say (again) *how* your claim follows from your premises plus your observations.

V. Optionally, implications that follow from the claim's being correct.

Try to be as explicit as possible, and take pains to lead the reader by the hand; do not make the reader work to understand your paper. Write it so that no reasonable reader can misinterpret it, get lost, or otherwise fail to understand.

One last piece of advice. It ought not to be necessary to say this, but experience tells us it is. Be sure to stick to the point: irrelevant claims, asides, speculations, facts, no matter how much you may think they display your brilliance or erudition, are not only unnecessary, but distracting. They not only lead the reader away from your argument and the point you are trying to make, but may induce an attempt to infer some relevance of them to your claim. When this fails, the reader may, in irritation, infer something you don't intend. But if you can't refrain from indulging in this, clearly label speculations or asides as such, and/or relegate them to footnotes.

4.2   A Note on Citations

The *Language* style sheet (published annually in the LSA Bulletin by the Linguistic Society of America) spells out the forms that are standard in linguistics for both data citation and reference citation. Essentially, cited forms (morphemes, words, sentences) should be underlined or italicized when they appear in the text, OR set off by indentation, and numbered. It is a good idea to avoid treating numbered examples as sentence constituents. Instead, refer to the examples by number, and place them immediately following the sentence referring to them. Try to avoid beginning a sentence with an example number (as in (1d)), because it cannot be capitalized; if you want to have a reference to a numbered example as the subject of a sentence, forms using a classifier like *Example* or *Sentence* make your prose easier to process, and making a claim about the whole class of sentences that the example represents (as in (2d)) makes a stronger claim as well.

Examples of Inconsiderate References

1a. We can show that what is not a relative pronoun
    in standard English.
    (*Cited form not set off by punctuation*)

1b. Nonetheless, examples like Chris is easy for
    Sandy to please are acceptable.
    (*Cited form not set off by punctuation*)

1c. Contrary to their hypothesis, examples like (37)
    37. Chris is easy for Sandy to please.
    are fully acceptable.
    (*Numbered example treated as sentence constituent*)

1d. (37) is fully acceptable.
    (*Sentence beginning with non-alphabetic character*)

Clearer References

2a. We can show that *what* is not a relative pronoun
    in standard English.

2b. Nonetheless, examples like (7) are acceptable.

    7. Chris is easy for Sandy to please.

2c. Example (37) is fully acceptable.

2d. Sentences like (37) are fully acceptable.

If a cited form is from a foreign language, or if senses of a form are being distinguished, glosses should be given immediately after the cited form, and should be in single quotes. In citing data longer than a single morpheme from languages other than English, expressions should be set off by indentation, numbered, and provided with both a morpheme-by-morpheme gloss, and a free translation, as in (3).

3. Arm-a   vir-um-que   can-o
weapons-ACCpl man-ACCsg-and sing-1sgPRES
I sing of arms and the man

In-text references to other research generally follow the pattern used in this book. Form (4a) is most commonly used; form (4b) is used where specific page references are relevant.

4a. **Author[s] (Year)** (*E.g.*: Gazdar, Pullum, and Sag (1982))

4b. **Author[s] (Year: Pages)** (*E.g.*: Grice (1975: 41))

If two works by the same author from the same year are being cited in the same text, they are distinguished by lower-case letters immediately following the year.

At the end of the text, an alphabetical list of references should be provided. The basic forms of reference are given in (5).

5a. Lastname, Firstname. Year. Book-Title. Place of publication: Publisher.

5b. Lastname, Firstname. Year. Article-Title. Journalname Volumenumber: Pages.

5c. Lastname, Firstname. Year. Chapter-Title. Anthologyname, ed. by Editorsnames, Pages. Place: Publisher.

Consult the *Language* style sheet for complete details. There are two schools of thought on providing authors' full first names, as opposed to merely their initials. Some maintain that providing distinguishing initials only is an egalitarian and anti-sexist gesture. (Apparently, the assumption is that some readers will discount the validity of a reference they have never seen on the basis of the sex of the author, as inferred from the first name.) Others point out that failing to provide full first names of authors is inconsiderate and makes finding books referred to difficult if the reader does not already know the author's or editor's full name.

Footnotes (numbered consecutively through the text) are reserved for tangential observations, arguments, and explanations. Some authors indicate in footnotes data and observations that their analysis does not provide an account of. Some others may do this within the text itself. In either case, it is a highly commendable practice, as it (a) relieves the reader of the difficult problem of trying to figure out how the analysis accounts for things that it does not in fact account for, and (b) provides a focus for further research to either improve the analysis, or show that it is incapable in principle of accounting for such facts.

In published papers there is often an initial, unnumbered footnote acknowledging financial, intellectual, and/or moral support or assistance (including that of language consultants) which enabled the completion of the work in its present state.

5   THE SO-CALLED STANDARD THEORY

> Those who do not remember the
> past are condemned to repeat it.
> — *George Santayana*[1]

It is difficult to fully understand the goals and assumptions of current theories of syntax without some understanding of the so-called Standard Theory out of which they developed. Virtually no one today holds all of those goals and assumptions, or frames analyses in that theory, and it is mainly taught as a foil for introducing current theories.[2] Most aspects of the Standard Theory survive in one or another of the successor theories, and its present status notwithstanding, many influential linguists continue to write as if their audiences were familiar with it, so some acquaintance with Standard Theory analyses and arguments is essential for understanding much current work. One of the goals of this chapter and the following one is to make that work accessible to linguists who did not live through the development of the Standard Theory, and did not learn syntax from linguists who did.

The term *standard theory* actually refers not to a particular, fully articulated theory, but to the set of assumptions and hypotheses about the form of an adequate syntactic theory that is described in *Aspects of the Theory of Syntax* (Chomsky 1965). These were developed in the period 1960–1964 as the very small community of generative syntacticians worked to extend and refine the theory of generative grammar described in *Syntactic Structures* (Chomsky 1957). Bach (1974) and Akmajian and Heny (1975) provide detailed introductions.

---

[1] Anyone who doubts this has only to compare analyses written in the Government and Binding (GB) framework and its successors with analyses from the Generative Semantics branch of classical transformational grammar, reviled fifteen to twenty years earlier by proponents of GB's predecessors. Pullum (1989) provides an initial summary, and Jackendoff (in prep.), a more recent perspective.

[2] In fact, when the term *standard theory* was first used by Chomsky (Chomsky 1971), the set of assumptions and claims that it referred to had already been rejected by many linguists. As Kuhn's (1970) account of the development of scientific theories predicts, later theories were developed in an effort to improve on the account provided by the Standard Theory.

The Standard Theory of generative syntax assumed that context-free phrase-structure rules generated a set of initial constituent structures, represented as single-rooted, labelled, oriented, acyclic, directed graphs, headed by the initial symbol S. That is, they generated constituent-structure diagrams ("trees") rooted in S: referring to the graphs as labelled means that each non-terminal node has a category label; *directed* and *oriented* mean that domination and precedence are defined as antisymmetric relations on nodes; *acyclic* means that no node can immediately or ultimately dominate itself. A lexical insertion transformation[3] completed the definition of well-formed underlying structures by allowing the attachment of lexical items whose category specifications were consistent with the lexical categories which constituted the terminal elements of the constituent structure representations. These well-formed underlying structures (**deep structures** if they underlay well-formed surface structures)[4] were supposed to serve as input both to an interpretive semantic component, and to the transformations, which would define a class of well-formed surface structures. These, in turn, were supposed to be the input to the set of phonological rules which would provide phonetic representations for syntactically well-formed sentences.

5.1 The Base Component

In the *Aspects* description of the Standard Theory, the base component was a set of ordered rewriting rules (Chomsky 1957, 1965). A minority viewpoint was that underlying structures were defined by a set of **node admissibility conditions** (i.e., filters; McCawley 1968a) such that the node admissibility condition $A \rightarrow B\ C$ was interpreted as follows: a **local subtree** (that is, a mother and its constituent daughters) that is rooted in a node labelled A is well-formed if A dominates daughters labelled B and C, and B precedes C. A (non-local) tree was defined as well-formed if and only if every node in it was licensed by some such condition. Node admissibility conditions could be expressed with the same notation as phrase structure rules interpreted as rewriting rules; they were just interpreted differently. Interestingly, the minority viewpoint is the one which has prevailed, in that it is accepted by most of the current theories which take constituent structure as a primitive concept.

---

[3]For a critique of this idea and its descendants in more current theory, see Jackendoff (in preparation).

[4]An underlying structure could be well-formed with respect to the rules of the base component and lexical insertion, and still fail to underlie any well-formed surface structure, e.g.: [$_S$ [$_{NP}$ The child [$_S$ the ambassador attended a party]] [$_{VP}$ slept]].

5.2 Transformational Rules

Most attention was given to developing theories of transformations, that is, constraints on how their great descriptive potential could be restricted to just what was necessary to describe natural languages. This meant constraining what could and what could not be a possible transformation in a grammar of a natural language. One such restriction was that the analysis of the domain of a transformation was supposed to be limited to conditions that could be stated in terms of 'equals', 'not', 'and', and 'or', and combinations of these (**Boolean conditions on analyzability**). Thus, terms in an analysis could be described as having or lacking some property, or having two or more particular properties simultaneously, or having any of two or more critical properties, but quantificational expressions (*some, every, second, antepenultimate, ...*) were supposed to be excluded from the description of transformations. Some linguists felt that these restrictions were not strong enough, because they still allowed indefinitely complex transformations, and so, failed to exert pressure to search for optimal generalizations. In practice, even these restrictions were fairly widely ignored.

In the Standard Theory, transformational operations were limited to substitution and adjunction. Both were assumed to be defined for both categories and features, and for both constants (including the null string) and typed variables. Thus, the repertoire of allowed operations included:

- **insertion** (adjunction of a constant or a copy of some term A as a sister of some other term B)[5]

- **deletion** of a term (substitution by the null string)

- **movement** (adjunction of a copy of some term A, accompanied by substitution of the null string for that term)

- **feature-changing** and **feature-copying** (substitution of one feature specification for a null specification or for a different specification)

Thus, the conventional notation consisted of two parts. A **structural analysis** (or **structural description**, or **structural index**, abbreviated SD) specified an exhaustive analysis of a phrase-structure in terms of category-types and variables (place-holders for arbitrary sequences of category representations. A **structural change** (SC) was supposed to determine a corresponding structure

---

[5] **Chomsky-adjunction** (insertion of A as a sister to B_i with a new node labelled B dominating just A and B_i) was also proposed, but rejected by Chomsky (for syntax) until long after the Standard Theory was only a historical artifact.

in terms of the above-mentioned transformational operations on specified types, as in the representation of the passive transformation in (1).

1.

	X	–	NP	–	Aux	–	V	–	NP	–	Y
SD:	1		2		3		4		5		6
SC:	1		5		3+*be* + -*en*		4		*by*+2		6

This representation assumes a constituent structure of the sort indicated in (2), and says that passive structures differ from their active counterparts in that a copy of the NP which comes after the V in the active structure is substituted for the NP preceding the Aux, and a constituent consisting of the word *by* and a copy of the pre-Aux NP is substituted for the post-V NP, and that *be* and passive-participle morphology are sisters of the Aux node (or, in other formulations, sisters of nodes dominated by the Aux node).

(2)

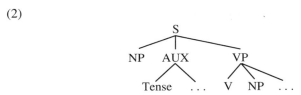

It was assumed that there were general principles which would entail that specifying the resultant string order would unambiguously indicate derived constituent structure (which, according to the Standard Theory did not need to conform to the rules of the base component, however they were construed). However, no such principles were ever articulated, and without them, resultant constituent structure was not unambiguously defined (see Borkin et al. 1971, Akmajian and Heny 1975, and McCawley 1978a for relevant discussion).

5.3 The Lexicon

The lexicon was taken to be a compendium of syntactic, semantic, morphological, and phonological information, organized (it was never clear exactly how) by lexical item (roughly: word or morpheme). Thus, for each lexical item there would be an indication of its syntactic category (possibly including a representation of its **subcategorization** requirements[6]— cf. Chomsky 1965), its underlying phonological representation in an appropriate notation, its meaning, and any morphological irregularities it was heir to.

---

[6]That is, a description of what sorts of phrases it allowed as sisters. This sort of information is necessary to allow distinctions among categories (such as transitive verb, intransitive verb, etc.) at the same time as generalizations about a category to which they all belong (verb).

5.4 Semantic Interpretation Rules

The semantic interpretive component was no more than a gleam in the eye during the period when the Standard Theory was dominant. As theories derived from it developed, particular principles of interpretation were proposed, but no general theory, and no general account of the meaning-bearing properties of linguistic expressions (cf. Jackendoff 1972 for discussion of many relevant matters). The absence of attention to interpretation in the Standard Theory was a major factor in the popularity of Generative Semantics (cf. McCawley 1968b, McCawley 1971b, Lakoff 1971) and Montague grammar (cf. Montague 1970, 1973, and for an introduction, Dowty, Wall, and Peters 1981) as alternatives to the Standard Theory and its extensions in the late 1960s and early 1970s.

5.5 The Phonological Component

As the Standard Theory was being articulated, a very explicit theory of phonological rules was being developed by Chomsky and Halle (Chomsky and Halle 1968), and it was assumed that the surface structures generated by a generative syntax would represent exactly what was relevant for phonological rules: for each terminal node, a representation of its underlying phonological segments, its category, and the category of each constituent of which it was a part (i.e., a representation of the constituent structure of its grammatical context).

5.6 Rule Interaction

The Standard Theory assumed (without explicit justification) that transformations "applied" in a fixed order (Chomsky 1957, 1965), though various other possibilities such as random sequential application (Pyle 1972) and simultaneous application (Koutsoudas 1972, 1973, Pullum 1979) were explored as well. Fixed ordering in a grammar is a blocking device, excluding as ungrammatical those derivations in which the rules apply in an order defined not to be allowed. In some versions the ordering was **total**, that is, with an ordering relation between every pair of transformations in the grammar; in other versions ordering was **partial**, so that ordering relations held between some pairs of transformations, but not all.

Transformations are sometimes described as feeding or bleeding one another. If two transformations T_1 and T_2 are in a feeding relation, then structures that match the structural change of T_1 (but not its structural description) also match the structural description of T_2, so that (metaphorically) T_1 creates input to T_2, hence **feeds** it. If T_1 **bleeds** T_2, then structures that match the structural description of T_2 also match the structural description of T_1, but not the structural change of T_1. So T_1 eliminates potential input to T_2, hence bleeds it. For example, in Standard Theory analyses Raising-to-object feeds Passive, and bleeds Equi-NP-deletion.

The terms *intrinsic* and *extrinsic* are also used to describe ordering relations. Transformational rules were said to be **intrinsically ordered** if the structural description of one rule would never be met unless the other rule had applied. Thus Passive would be intrinsically ordered before a rule of Agent-deletion, since the structural description of Agent-deletion could never be met except as a result of Passive.[7]

Rules can be in a feeding relationship in a derivation without being intrinsically ordered. For example, rule A (e.g., Passive) could apply to the lowest clause to feed rule B (e.g., Raising to Object) on the next higher clause, and still be ordered after rule B. If all rules were intrinsically ordered with respect to each other, there would be no need to state any ordering in a grammar, since the order of application would be determined entirely by syntactic structure and perhaps other principles like the principle of cyclic application (see Section 7 below).

Transformational rules were said to be **extrinsically ordered** when application in one order generates grammatical sentences, but application in the other order generates ungrammatical sentences. For example, it was argued that the passive rule and Lees and Klima's reflexive rule (Lees and Klima 1963) were extrinsically ordered because the order <Passive, Reflexive>, but not the order <Reflexive, Passive>, defines grammatical sentences:

---

[7]Strictly speaking, these two rules are ordered intrinsically only if the only *by*-phrases that can meet the structural description of Agent-deletion are those which arise via Passive. If *by*-phrases like those in (i) can be in the passive VP, and not outside it, and Agent-deletion only refers to structural properties of a phrase-marker, (that is, does not refer to grammatical relations or thematic roles), then Agent-deletion would be ordered after Passive extrinsically, not intrinsically, because *by*-phrases in such base-generated structures as underlie (i) would satisfy the structural description of Agent-deletion.

ia. The dog was sleeping by something.

ib. Elizabeth was crowned by something [i.e., next to something] by the Archbishop of Canterbury.

JOHN$_i$ KILLED JOHN$_i$

| Psv: | JOHN$_i$ WAS KILLED BY JOHN$_i$ | (*Passive*) |
| Rxv: | John was killed by himself. | (*Reflexive*) |

JOHN$_i$ KILLED JOHN$_i$

| Rxv: | JOHN$_i$ KILLED HIMSELF$_i$ | (*Reflexive*) |
| Psv: | *Himself was killed by John. | (*Passive*) |

It was often assumed, on the basis of analyses such as the ones assumed in that argument, that not all rules were intrinsically ordered, and that some extrinsic ordering statements were necessary. In the early 1970s, linguists began to search for alternative principles to explain these sorts of facts. It is easy to see why extrinsic ordering statements were found unsatisfying and non-explanatory; although extrinsic ordering was taken for granted as a descriptive device, in fact extrinsic ordering statements add considerably to the complexity of a grammar. To postulate an extrinsic ordering is to claim that there is no explanation for the facts that motivate the ordering relation; this implies that an extrinsic ordering statement is an idiosyncratic fact about the grammar that speakers must learn in the course of learning the language.

No current theory assumes fixed ordering. All seek to explain the facts that extrinsic ordering was thought necessary for by means of other principles.

5.7 The Principle of Cyclic Application of Transformations

Given the Standard Theory assumption of fixed order among transformations, cyclic rule application was proposed as a solution to a paradox that arose in determining what the fixed sequence must be (Fillmore 1963). It was observed that in certain cases, it appears that rule A applies before rule B, but in others, it appears that B applies before A. If the order in which rules apply is always the same, this would not be possible. Hence there was an apparent rule-ordering paradox. It could be resolved by assuming that the rules are ordered so that one precedes the other, but they apply in a cyclic fashion.

Cyclic application means that all transformations apply, in their order, first to the lowest S in the tree, then to the next higher S and everything it dominates, then to the next higher than that, and so on. In this way, if A is ordered before B, in any given cyclic domain, A always applies before B, but B could apply before A in a particular derivation, if the first application of B is on a lower cycle than the first application of A. The appearance of B applying before an application of A follows from the two applications being in different cyclic domains. As an illustration, in the derivation of sentences like

John believes Fred to have been described by Mary, Passive applies before Raising, as shown in the derivation in (3), even though Raising is ordered before Passive.

Derivation I

(3a)

First (S$_2$) cycle: Raising does not apply (S.D. is not met); Passive applies:

(3b)

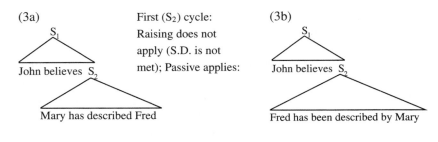

(3c)   Second (S$_1$) cycle: Raising applies; Passive (optional) does not apply.

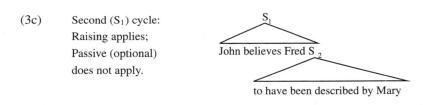

Cyclic application in a phrase-marker with embedded clauses is represented schematically in the following diagram. The rules 1–5 apply first, in that order, to the most deeply embedded S, S$_3$. They then apply, again in order, taking the next higher S, S$_2$, as their domain. Then they apply again, again in order, taking as their domain the next higher S, and so on, for however many clauses (nodes labelled S) the phrase-marker contains.

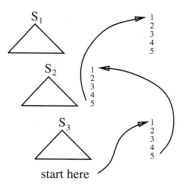

Diagram I: Cyclic Application

Thus, in the derivation of the sentence *Kim is believed by the Feds to be presumed to be elected*, Raising and Passive were argued to apply cyclically, first to the lowest S, then both to the next S up, and so on. There is no other obviously motivated way to explain how *Kim*, the underlying object in S_3, can be the subject of S_1.

Derivation II

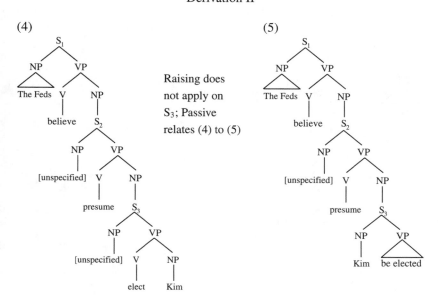

Raising on
S$_2$ relates
(5) to (6)

(6)

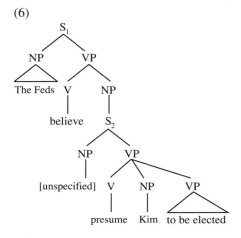

Passive on
S$_2$ relates
(6) to (7)

(7)

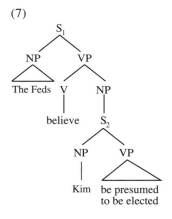

Raising applies
to S_1 to relate
(7) to (8)

(8)

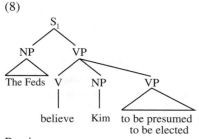

Passive on
S_1 relates
(8) to (9)

(9)

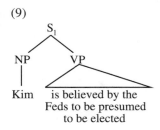

Similarly, in the derivation of *John believes himself to have proved himself to be innocent* from the structure given below,[8] Raising and Reflexivization

---

[8]The reduced acceptability of such sentences for some speakers is attributable to the presence of two coreferential reflexives. Exactly as bad as sentences with two true reflexives are sentences with a true reflexive and various kinds of emphatic reflexives (i–iii); sentences with two non-coreferential reflexives are unimpeachable (iv):

    i. ?The King himself shaves himself. (=Even the King...)
   ii. ?Myself, I want myself to win. (=Personally, I...)
  iii. ?John stabbed himself in the back himself. (=...with no help)
  iv. John considers himself to have persuaded Mary to bandage herself.

When two coreferential reflexives are (or are attached to) arguments of different verbs (as in v–vii), the sentence is more acceptable than *John believes himself to have proved himself to be innocent*.

    v. John considers himself the best judge of whether [he was able to amuse himself].
   vi. The King himself knows [that he is expected to shave himself].
  vii. I myself didn't want you to know [that I want myself to win].

must apply first on S_2. Only then are the structural descriptions met for them to apply on the main clause (S_1). In each case, the structural description for Reflexivization will not be met until Raising has applied.

It was widely assumed (cf. Chomsky 1965) that the principle of the cycle was a universal organizing principle of grammar, perhaps innate. It was an open question whether it was an independent principle, or a consequence of some other principle or principles (e.g., a principle favoring maximal application of rules, or the Extended Standard Theory's principle of subjacency).[9] There is now little doubt that the facts that motivated it are a consequence of more general principles, and the question that is debated is: Which principles?

Derivation III

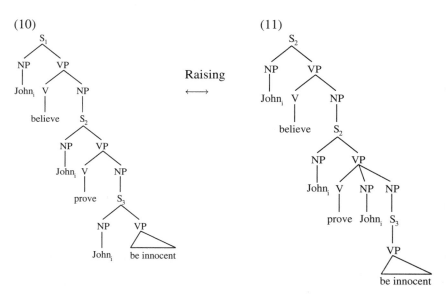

---

[9]The principle of **subjacency** prohibits the movement of any element to a site more than one bounding node above. For present purposes, the only bounding node is S, although strictly speaking, NP is also a bounding node in this theory. For further details, see Chomsky 1977.

Reflexive
relates
(11) to (12)

Raising
relates
(12) to (13)

(12)

(13)

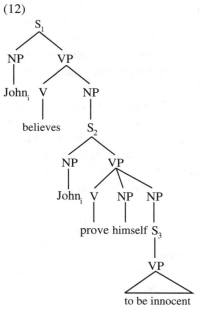

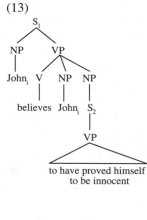

(14)

Reflexive
relates
(13) to (14)

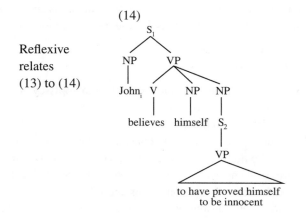

5.8 Classes of Rules

Not all rules appeared to have to apply in a successive cyclic fashion. In some articulations of the Standard Theory, there were rules that applied only once, taking as their domain the entire phrase-marker. If one or more cyclic rules had to apply after one of these rules, the rules that preceded the cyclic rule(s) were called **last-cyclic**—they applied on the last cycle, interspersed with cyclic rules. Non-cyclic rules whose application never, in any derivation, preceded the application of any cyclic rule, were called **post-cyclic**—they applied after all cyclic applications.

Post-cyclic and last-cyclic rules both took the whole phrase-marker as their domain, and neither applied before the cyclic rules had applied to all embedded clauses. The difference was that last-cyclic rules were, by definition, cyclic rules, and so, applied among the cyclic rules on the highest S. But they were cyclic rules whose structural descriptions were met only in the highest clause of the tree, so presumably some ordinary cyclic rules might be ordered after some last-cyclic rules.

Post-cyclic rules, on the other hand, would not apply before all of the cyclic rules had applied in every clause, including the highest. No cyclic rule could ever apply after any post-cyclic rule. An ordered list of rules in a grammar with last-cyclic rules is represented schematically in (15), with the asterisk indicating that the rule applies on the last cycle only.

15. 1, 2, 3, *4, 5, *6, *7, 8, 9

An ordered list of rules in a grammar with post-cyclic rules strictly separates the post-cyclic from the cyclic rules, as represented schematically in (16).

16. 1, 2, 3, 4, 5 (Cyclic rules)
     6, 7, 8, 9 (Post-cyclic rules)

Some linguists reasoned that since some rules had to apply cyclically, meta-theoretical considerations entailed that all rules should be considered to be cyclic. Other linguists concluded that metatheoretical considerations entailed that only those rules which had to be considered cyclic because they feed other cyclic rules should be considered cyclic. These linguists considered all rules which never feed any cyclic rule to be post-cyclic. See Postal (1972) and Chomsky (1973) for some discussion of this and related issues.

One rule which took an entire phrase-marker as its domain, Sentence Pronominalization, was argued (Lakoff 1966) to be **pre-cyclic**, because it appeared to have to apply before any cyclic rules. It was also proposed (Ross 1970a) that some rules, called "anywhere rules", could apply, or would have to apply, at any stage of a derivation where their structural descriptions were met.

6 DEVELOPING CONSTRAINTS ON POSSIBLE DESCRIPTIONS

6.1 Island Constraints

In Standard Theory analyses, numerous rules were described as "applying over a variable," affecting elements indefinitely far away, and creating **unbounded dependency constructions**, constructions where elements dependent on each other could be indefinitely far apart. The use of the technical term *variable* is not gratuitous; variables are crucial to the correct formulation of some syntactic rules, given Standard Theory assumptions about the nature and form of syntactic rules. In the context of transformational rules, variables are symbols whose reference ranges over sequences of nodes derivable according to the grammar, including a null sequence. Thus, the transformation for the unbounded constituent question construction would contain variables since the question word, which has a fixed position in surface structure, can originate anywhere in the constituent structure of the sentence. In the notation that was conventional, this WH-Movement rule was formulated roughly as in (1).

1.   X – NP[+WH] – Y
          1   2   3
  → 2 1   0   3

In this example, the variables are written as X and Y; by convention, upper case letters from the end of the Latin alphabet are used to represent variables over sequences of constituents. The following trees, analyzed according to the structural description in (1), show how the reference of X and Y varies.

2a.

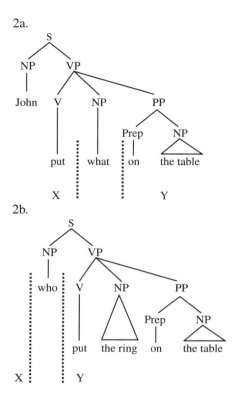

2b.

2c.

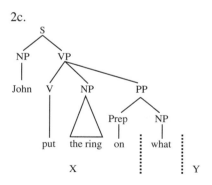

Notice that X in (2b) and Y in (2c) refer to a null sequence, and that what X refers to in (2a) and (2c) is not even a constituent.

Two kinds of variables were distinguished, abbreviatory variables and essential variables, although the traditional notation does not differentiate between them. **Abbreviatory variables** stood for a finite listing of constituent types and sequences of constituent types which could intervene among the elements crucially affected by the rule. Thus, abbreviatory variables were not essential to the formulation of the rule; any rule containing abbreviatory variables could be formulated without them, with a listing in place of each variable. An example of a rule containing an abbreviatory variable is Relative Clause Extraposition, proposed to account for sentences like (3).

3a. A balloon blew up which I had bought.

3b. I gave a balloon to my brother which I had bought.

3c. I gave the man some balloons who was going to take the children to the zoo.

3d. I blew the balloon up which I had bought.

3e. I blew up the balloon yesterday which I bought in Vienna.

3f. He painted the house purple that used to be such a nice brown color.

The relative clause that belongs with any NP in a clause may appear at the end of the clause, but there are a finite number of places for an NP in a simple clause, so the rule would not have to be written with a variable, as in (4).[1] It could be written with a disjunctive listing in the description of the structure it applies to, as in (5).

4. $\text{X} - _{NP}[\text{NP S}] - \text{Y}$
   $\quad 1 \qquad\quad 2\ 3\ \ 4$
   $\quad 1 \qquad\quad 2\ 0\ \ 4\,3$

5.
$$\left\{ \begin{matrix} 0 \\ \text{NP V} \end{matrix} \right\} - _{NP}[\text{NP S}] - \left\{ \begin{matrix} \text{VP} \\ \text{PrepP} \\ \text{NP} \\ \text{Prtcl} \\ \text{Adv} \\ \text{AdjP} \end{matrix} \right\}$$

$\qquad\quad 1 \qquad\quad\ 2\ \ 3 \qquad\quad 4$
$\rightarrow\quad 1 \qquad\quad\ 2\ \ 0 \qquad\quad 4\ \ 3$

---

[1] Strictly speaking, the formulation in (4) is valid only with the additional information that Extraposition from NP is upper-bounded (see p. 88). This means that it does not allow the material intervening between the extraposed relative clause and its head to contain an S-node; i.e., it cannot "move" the relative clause out of the clause it originates in. Several formulations in this chapter violate the Standard Theory stipulation that structural descriptions be just string analyses, and not include indication of bracketing. Formulating transformational rules perspicuously under this constraint turned out to be fraught with difficulty, and may well have been a factor in Chomsky's opting to develop transformational grammar in the direction of reducing the size and role of the transformational component (Chomsky 1969, 1973, 1977, 1981).

Either of these formulations will account for relative clause extrapositions in the sentences in (3). The formulation in (4) is more concise, but both adequately describe the extrapositions.

On the other hand, there are rules in the formulation of which the use of variables is essential;[2] such rules could not be correctly formulated in the Standard Theory without the use of variables. Examples of rules with **essential variables** are the WH-Movement rules proposed to account for relative clauses and constituent questions, and the Topicalization rule, which allows a constituent to appear at the beginning of the sentence, instead of where it would be expected to go. In these cases, it is not possible to abbreviate the varying structural description with a finite listing. The relative clause rule provides a perspicuous example. Written with variables, it looks something like (6):

6. $\text{X} - {}_{NP}[\text{NP} \, {}_{S}[\text{Y} - \text{NP[+rel]} - \text{Z}] \,] - \text{W}$
        1   2   3 4   5   6
   → 1   2   4 3 0   5   6

Rule (6) says that a structure with a relative pronoun may be adjacent in a derivation to a structure that is identical except that the pronoun is between the head NP and the relative clause, rather than within the relative clause. All of the variables in (6) are essential variables. The variables X and W ensure that the rule applies to relative clauses at any depth of embedding in a sentence. The variables Y and Z ensure that it applies to a relative pronoun at any position within the relative clause, regardless (this is most crucial) of how deeply it may be embedded within the relative clause. To write (6) without variables, merely to account for the four sentences of (7), one would have to start out with a rule like (8):

7a. The man who Dale saw is my uncle.

7b. The man who Jan thinks Dale saw is my uncle.

7c. The man who Jan thinks saw Dale is my uncle.

7d. I know a man who Sam says Jan thinks Dale saw.

---

[2]Essential, that is, if unbounded "movement" is described by a single invocation of a transformational rule, as it is in Ross's work. Formulations in the Extended Standard Theory (Chomsky 1973, 1981) get the effect of unbounded movement by successive cyclic application within a bounded domain. In non-transformational theories, there is no "movement", and the unbounded nature of the dependency is described by other means (cf. Chapter 7 for some discussion).

8.

$$
\begin{bmatrix} \left\{ \begin{matrix} 0 \\ NP\ V \end{matrix} \right\}_{NP} & NP \begin{bmatrix} \begin{bmatrix} \left\{ \begin{matrix} NP\ V \\ NP\ V\ [NP\ V \\ NP\ V\ [NP\ V\ [NP\ V \end{matrix} \right\} \end{bmatrix}_S - NP - \left\{ \begin{matrix} 0 \\ VP \end{matrix} \right\} \end{bmatrix} \end{bmatrix} - \left\{ \begin{matrix} VP \\ 0 \end{matrix} \right\}
$$

1	2	3	4	5	6
→ 1	2 4 3		0	5	6

And even this rule will not account for the relative clauses in (9).

9a. The man who saw Dale is my uncle.
9b. Sara said she knew a man who Dale hired.
9c. The man who I gave a dime to was drunk.
9d. The man who I'm sure Sam said Jan thinks Dale saw will be here soon.

To account for them, a different alternative must be added for each sentence, so the WH-Movement rule would have to be formulated as in (10).

10.

$$
\left\{ \begin{matrix} 0 \\ NP\ V \\ NP\ V\ NP\ V \end{matrix} \right\} - \begin{bmatrix} NP - \begin{bmatrix} \begin{bmatrix} \left\{ \begin{matrix} 0 \\ NP\ V \\ NP\ V\ NP\ V \\ NP\ V\ NP\ V\ NP\ V \\ NP\ V\ NP\ V\ NP\ V\ NP\ V \\ NP\ V\ NP\ Prep \end{matrix} \right\} - NP - \left\{ \begin{matrix} VP \\ 0 \end{matrix} \right\} \end{bmatrix}_S \end{bmatrix}_{NP} \end{bmatrix} \left\{ \begin{matrix} VP \\ 0 \end{matrix} \right\}
$$

1	2	3	4	5	6
→ 1	2 4	3	0	5	6

It should be clear that no matter how long the listings for these variables get, it is easy to find a sentence with a deeper level of embedding which will make it necessary to make them longer. Thus, essential variables stand for an infinite number of sequences, and cannot be represented by a finite listing. Rules with this property must be written with variables.

But the use of variables leads to a new dilemma. On the one hand, without the use of variables, the rules in question cannot be formulated in a way that expresses all the possible domains to which the rule must refer. But the formulations with variables are too strong. They predict that the rule applies in cases where it would generate impossible sentences. Since a variable stands for an arbitrary sequence of elements, to use variables in a rule is to claim that the rule has an unlimited domain. But many rules affecting elements indefinitely far down in a tree do not actually have unlimited domains. For example, the WH-Movement rule for relative clauses cannot apply to the *who* in structure (11a), and the similar question rule cannot apply to the *what* in structure (12a).

11a. THE MAN [I SPOKE ABOUT WHO AND HIS DAUGHTERS] IS GOING TO FRANCE

11b. *The man who I spoke about and his daughters is going to France.

12a. LOU BOUGHT A BOOK [WHICH DESCRIBED THE HISTORY OF ?WHAT]

12b. *What did Lou buy a book which described the history of?

Chomsky (1964) tried to reconcile the indefinitely large domains of these rules with observed restrictions on them by means of a principle which came to be known as the **A-over-A principle**:

> if the phrase X of a category A is embedded within a larger phrase ZXW which is also of category A, then no rule applying to the category A applies to X (but only to ZXW).

This principle says that in a structure like (13), transformations which affect (e.g., reorder, redefine) A must affect the topmost (boxed) A, not the dominated (circled) A.

13.

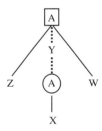

The A-over-A principle proved to be too strong, however. It predicted that certain sentences which were grammatical could not be generated. For example, in relating (14) to a structure like (15), the rule applies to the dominated (circled) NP, not the dominating (boxed) NP.

14. What are you uncertain about giving _ to John?

15.

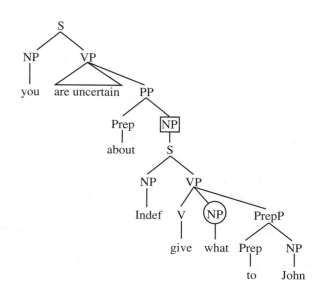

Yet (14) does not have the ungrammaticality of (11b) and (12b) which the A-over-A principle predicts. This led Ross to re-examine the phenomena which the A-over-A principle was supposed to account for. The result of his re-examination was a landmark dissertation, *Constraints on variables in syntax* (Ross 1967). Ross argued that the A-over-A principle, and weaker conditions proposed by Chomsky, which dictated the interpretation of category labels in rules, should be replaced by a set of constraints on the interpretation of essential variables in syntactic rules. Of these constraints, he argued that two, the Complex NP Constraint and the Coordinate Structure Constraint, were universal, and several others held in specific languages. The contents of some of these constraints are given below, with illustrations.

(I) **The Complex NP Constraint** (CNPC): No element in an S dominated by an NP with a lexical head may be moved out of that NP.[3]
This includes relative clauses such as (16) below, where identical subscripts indicate coreference, as well as clauses in apposition to nouns like *fact, claim, idea,* etc., as in (17).

---

[3]To preserve the simplicity and flavor of the constraints as formulated in 1967, the dynamic metaphors have not been edited out.

16.   17.

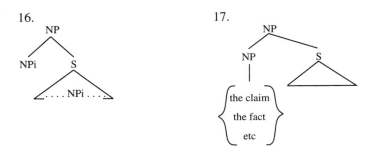

Thus, the CNPC precludes the following (partial) derivations. (We adopt the convention of representing partial derivations by means of a schematic representation (in small capital letters) of a structure that meets the structural description of a rule (the "input" to the rule, in that unfortunate metaphor) connected by means of an arrow to a string of words that has the properties of the structural change of the rule (the "output" of the rule).[4] The X-arrow symbol ($-X\rightarrow$) is used in illustrations to indicate that the two structures are not related by the rule in question.

MO MET A MAN WHO EATS ?WHAT $-X\rightarrow$ *What did Mo meet a man who eats?

JO BELIEVES THE CLAIM THAT ?WHO EATS GREEN TOMATOES $-X\rightarrow$ *Who does Jo believe the claim that eats green tomatoes?

BO MET A PLAYER WHO EATS MARIGOLDS $-X\rightarrow$ *Marigolds, Bo met a player who eats.

DANA HEARD A CLAIM THAT SAM EATS MARIGOLDS $-X\rightarrow$ *Marigolds, Dana heard a claim that Sam eats.

THE BOOKS [DALE MET THE PLAYER WHO OWNS WHICH] WERE GOOD $-X\rightarrow$ *The books which Dale met the player who owns were good.

THE BOOKS [JAN IS SUSPICIOUS OF THE CLAIM THAT DALE WROTE WHICH] WERE GOOD $-X\rightarrow$

---

[4]The arrow represents a relation of well-formedness between adjacent representations in a derivation, and must not be misconstrued as making any claims about speech production.

*The books which Jan is suspicious of the claim that Dale wrote were good.

(II) **Coordinate Structure Constraint** (CSC): No conjunct may be moved, nor any element contained within a conjunct.

JOHN NOMINATED ?WHO AND DALE −X→ *Who did John nominate and Dale?

JOAN CHOSE DALE AND WHO −X→ *Who did Joan choose Dale and?

KIM DUSTED THE TABLES AND SWEPT ?WHAT −X→
*What did Kim dust the tables and sweep?

SANDY LIKES MIKE AND IKE −X→ *Ike, Sandy likes and Mike.
SANDY LIKES MIKE AND IKE −X→ *Mike, Sandy likes Ike and.

LOU WANTED TO TYPE LETTERS AND STAMP ENVELOPES −X→
*Envelopes, Lou wanted to type letters and stamp.

JO MET THE MAN [JAN INVITED WHO AND LOWE] −X→
*Jo met the man who Jan invited and Lowe.

JO MET THE MAN [JAN INVITED LOWE AND WHO] −X→
*Jo met the man who Jan invited Lowe and.

MO LIKED THE BEANS [JO COOKED WHICH AND THEIR UNCLE COOKED THE POTATOES] −X→
*Mo liked the beans, which Joan cooked and their uncle cooked the potatoes.

An element can be "extracted" from both (or all) conjuncts (**across-the-board** extraction):

SAM SEALED THE ENVELOPES AND JAN STAMPED THE ENVELOPES
→ The envelopes, Sam sealed and Jan stamped.

Likewise:

What did Sam lick __ and Jan stamp __?
The envelopes which Sam licked __ and Jan stamped __ got lost.

(III) **Sentential Subject Constraint** (SSC): No element can be moved out of an S which is the subject of a higher S.

> [THE PLUMBER'S GREEDILY EATING ?WHAT] ANNOYED CHRIS
> —X→ *What did the plumber's greedily eating annoy Chris?

> [THAT THE PLUMBER ATE ?WHAT] ANNOYED CHRIS —X→
> *What did that the plumber ate annoy Chris?

> [THE PLUMBER'S GREEDILY EATING TADPOLES] ANNOYED CHRIS
> —X→ *Tadpoles, the plumber's greedily eating annoyed Chris.

> [THAT THE PLUMBER ATE TADPOLES] ANNOYED CHRIS —X→
> *Tadpoles, that the plumber ate annoyed Chris.

> THESE ARE THE TADPOLES [[LOU'S EATING WHICH] ANNOYED CHRIS
> —X→ *These are the tadpoles which Lou's eating annoyed Chris.

> THESE ARE THE TADPOLES [[THAT LOU ATE WHICH] ANNOYED CHRIS]
> —X→ *These are the tadpoles which (that) Lou ate annoyed Chris.

If a clause which is the logical subject is not in subject position, but is extraposed to the end of its clause in accordance with the optional rule of Extraposition, it will support extraction:

> What did it annoy Chris that the plumber ate?
> Tadpoles, it annoyed Chris that the plumber ate.
> These are the tadpoles which it annoyed Chris that the plumber ate.

IV. **Left Branch Condition** (LBC): No NP which is the leftmost constituent of a larger NP can be reordered out of this NP.

> [WE ELECTED CHARLIE BROWN'S DOG PRESIDENT —X→
> *Charlie Brown's we elected dog president

> [WE ELECTED CHARLIE BROWN'S DOG PRESIDENT —X→
> *Charlie Brown we elected's dog president

Ross also observed that all rules which position an element over a variable to the right (e.g., Extraposition, Heavy NP Shift) are **upper-bounded**; that is, they cannot position the element beyond the end of the S it originates in. Linguists working within the Extended Standard Theory (following

Chomsky 1973, 1977) and its successors took the position that all rules are bounded in that they may re-position elements only within a single clause or within the next higher clause (Chomsky's principle of Subjacency[5]), and they revised their theoretical and descriptive principles accordingly, postulating, for example, that unbounded dependencies arise through successive bounded movements from complementizer position to complementizer position. Here, we use the predicate *unbounded* to describe unbounded dependency CON-STRUCTIONS; the reader should keep in mind that some theories treat all rules as strictly bounded, as described in Chapter 7.

Additional references. Morgan (1975) reviews a variety of phenomena which indicate that the **islands** (cf. Ross 1967) defined by Ross' constraints delimit the domain of a number of non-syntactic aspects of linguistic competence. Grosu (1972, 1973a, 1973b, 1974, 1975) explores the possibility of a unified psychological explanation for the constraints. Gazdar (1981) and Flickinger (1983) describe how their effects can be represented in a non-transformational version of generative grammar. Goldsmith (1985) and Lakoff (1986) demonstrate that the element clause of the Coordinate Structure Constrain is too strong, and argue that the relevant constraints are more likely pragmatic than syntactic.

6.2 Output Conditions

In the earliest days of generative grammar it was observed that there was an interaction between Dative Movement and Pronominalization which defined paradigms such as (18).

18a. They gave the boy the book.
18b. They gave the book to the boy.
18c. They gave him the book.
18d. They gave the book to him.
18e. *They gave the boy it.
18f. They gave it to the boy.
18g. ?*They gave him it.
18h. They gave it to him.

This and similar interactions between Particle Movement and Pronominalization (as in (19)), and between Inversion after directional adverbs and Pronominalization (as in (20)) led Ross (1967) to argue that it would miss a generalization to state separately that if the NP after which the prepositional

---

[5]See Footnote 9 of Chapter 5, and Chomsky 1973, 1977, and subsequent works for details and motivation.

phrase, particle, or verb was positioned was a pronoun, Particle Movement was obligatory, and Inversion and Dative Movement were blocked.[6]

19a. I put out the cat.

19b. I put the cat out.

19c. *I put out him.

19d. I put him out.

20a. The cat went out.

20b. Out went the cat.

20c. He went out.

20d. *Out went he.

What really seemed to be going on, he claimed, was that (18e), (18g), (19c), and (20d) were all grammatical in the technical sense of being generated by the grammar representing the speakers' competence, but that linguistic ability also includes the ability to judge that certain grammatical sentences were less acceptable than others, judgements which he argued were rule-governed in the general sense, and could be codified as conditions on the "output" of the grammar. Ross proposed the two output conditions in (21) and (22), and suggested that the second might be universal.

21. (= Ross' 3.41: Output condition on post-verbal constituents) The favored order for post-verbal constituents in English is:

1. Direct object pronouns

2a. Indirect object pronouns

2b. Demonstrative adjectives (*this*, *that* etc.) and integers used as pronouns (e.g., *two* in *give me two*)

3. Proper names, regardless of grammatical relation

4a. Particles

4b. Lexically-headed NPs with no postnominal modifiers, regardless of grammatical relation

5. Reduced directional phrases (e.g., *out* in *let out*)

6. The second object of double object verbs (e.g., *president* in *elect him president*)

7. Complement adjectives (e.g., *available* in *make them available*, *red* in *paint it red*)

8. Prepositional phrases functioning as indirect object phrases and directional phrases.

---

[6]Or that Particle Movement and Dative Movement were obligatory, assuming that Dative Movement "created" prepositional phrases instead of reducing them.

9. Non-complex NPs with postnominal modifiers (e.g., *something small*)
10. Complex NPs
11. Idiosyncratically phrase-final predicatives (e.g., *company* in *keep someone company, to* in *bring someone to*)

22. (= Ross' 3.27: a "general output condition on performance") Grammatical sentences containing an internal NP which exhaustively dominates S[7] are unacceptable.

This condition was intended to account for such contrasts as (23–25), where the (a) examples are analyzed as having an internal S exhaustively dominated by NP, the (b) examples as having an internal S not exhaustively dominated by NP, and the (c) examples as having a peripheral (non-internal) S dominated by NP.

23a. *Did [that John showed up] please you? (*internal S*)
23b. Did [[the fact] [that John showed up]] please you? (*S not exhaustively dominated by NP*)
23c. Did it please you [that John showed up]? (*S not internal*)

24a. ?*That that John showed up pleased her was obvious.
24b. That the fact that John showed up pleased her was obvious.
24c. That it pleased her that John showed up was obvious.

25a. ?*I want that Dale left to remain a secret.
25b. I want the fact that Dale left to remain a secret.
25c. I want it to remain a secret that Dale left.

The (a) sentences are clearly English, and nearly understandable, but clearly unacceptable.

In a dissertation finished a year later (and published in 1971), Perlmutter proposed that constraints or conditions on what constituted a well-formed surface structure might have to be part of the grammar itself. This contrasts with Ross' claim that the output conditions which he (Ross) discussed were

---

[7]That is, S is all it dominates. In the theory of phrase structure that Ross was assuming, a clause that had the grammatical relation of subject or direct object was represented as S dominated by NP.

extragrammatical,[8] and also with Chomsky's (1965) claim that such functions might be a part of linguistic metatheory (universal grammar), that is, constraints on what could be a well-formed surface structure in any language.

Specifically, Perlmutter (1971) argued that a transformational grammar of Spanish could not adequately describe the distribution of clitic pronouns without a **surface structure constraint** that excluded all sentences containing sequences of clitics not conforming to a certain pattern. No independent motivation could be found, he argued, for phrase structure rules and transformations which would guarantee correct clitic order; a filter was needed in addition to clitic-deriving rules and clitic-reordering rules.

In another chapter, he proposed that the grammars of both English and French contain the surface structure constraint in (26):

26. (= Perlmutter's (9), Chapter 4)
   Any sentence other than an Imperative in which there is an S that does not contain a subject in surface structure is ungrammatical. (1971:100)

(Schmerling (1973) discusses a constrained class of counterexamples to this, from colloquial English.)

The difference between Ross' proposals and Perlmutter's is that the sentences which Ross' proposals exclude are treated as being grammatical, but unacceptable, and to be accounted for by a theory of performance, pragmatics, or style, while the sentences excluded by Perlmutter's proposals are treated as ungrammatical (excluded by the grammar of a language), hence unacceptable. Since the acceptability judgements of native speakers which constitute the empirical basis for testing grammatical theories provide no insight into the source of the unacceptability, deciding whether a particular surface filter is part of the grammar, or an extragrammatical constraint on the use of certain is not testable directly, being more a question of which alternative contributes more to a single, internally consistent theory of grammar, and of which one allows a tighter characterization of universal grammar, and the like.

Some linguists (cf. Green 1981, 1982b) argue that if a construction excluded by a surface filter (or any other kind) would ever be the natural way to describe a state of affairs or event (holding constant the other linguistic conventions that are part of the grammar) then the filter must be wrong, and the construction must be treated as grammatical (i.e., generated by the grammar). When instances of the construction are judged to be unacceptable, their

---

[8] Actually, while Ross claimed that both 3.41 and 3.27 determined acceptability, not grammaticality, he suggested that 3.27 was extragrammatical in that it was universal, and thus a metatheoretical constraint on the notion of well-formed surface structure, while he treated 3.41 as a rule of English of a special kind, conflating 'grammatical' and 'acceptable', despite his claim in his footnote 8 that he was using those terms as defined by Chomsky (1965: Sec. 1.2).

unacceptability must arise from a contingent, extragrammatical constraint. Theories of some other linguists (cf. Chomsky 1969, 1977) provide for the possibility of ungrammatical but acceptable sentences, so both options would be open to them: treating the contingently acceptable sentences as grammatical but sometimes unacceptable, or as ungrammatical but sometimes acceptable.

A variety of phenomena, including pronominalization (Lakoff 1976), negative polarity items (Baker 1970), idioms (Green and Morgan 1976), and lexical items (Green 1974, Chapter 5) have received descriptions in terms of surface filters of one sort or another. Chomsky and Lasnik (1977) proposed filters to exclude validly derived occurrences of *that* before a site no longer occupied by a WH-element, and occurrences of *for* followed by *to*, as well as filters prohibiting doubly-filled COMP nodes and constituents analyzable as [NP *to* VP]. Surface filters have come to play an increasing role in generative grammar, and restrictions on individual rules and their interaction a much smaller one than was imagined when Ross and Perlmutter first introduced the notion in the late 1960s. This evolution is evident both in the Government and Binding framework (Chomsky 1981, and subsequent works) and in phrase-structure approaches to syntax (Gazdar, Klein, Pullum, and Sag 1985; Pollard and Sag 1987, 1994).

6.3   Other Kinds of Constraints on Derivations

As Lakoff (1970) pointed out, phrase structure rules and transformational rules (as well as deep- and surface-structure constraints) are local principles— phrase structure rules define conditions of well-formedness on underlying phrase markers one local subtree at a time, in terms of immediately dominating and immediately preceding constituents, and transformational rules define constraints on pairs of phrase-markers adjacent in a derivation. However, Lakoff went on to argue, sometimes transformational rules appear to require reference to more than two stages in a derivation, or to non-adjacent phrase markers. As he put it, transformations are global in nature, and cannot be stated, or stated perspicuously, as local relations. He noted, for instance, Postal's (1970) observation that the Equi-NP-Deletion rule invoked in the description of controlled verb phrases like *to compete* in sentences like *John is eager [ ] to compete* behaved in some respects like a cyclic rule, in that its structural description was in both a feeding and a bleeding relation (cf. Chapter 5) with other cyclic rules (namely, Passive and Raising). In other respects, Postal observed, it was like a post-cyclic rule: constraints on the deleted NP were predictable from the assumption that it was an anaphoric pronoun, and pronouns, Postal argued (citing facts about their configurational relations to their antecedents), had to be generated via a post-cyclic transformation. Consequently, Equi had to be postcyclic (or last-cyclic), in order to be able to follow a postcyclic rule. Assuming that Equi was last-cyclic would not account for the data that supported its being cyclic, and since, by definition, a rule could not be simultaneously cyclic and postcyclic, Postal was forced to claim that it was really two rules: a cyclic rule which in effect marked complement subjects which were coreferential to an NP in the next clause up with a special pronominal feature [+DOOM], and a post-cyclic rule which deleted DOOMed pronouns.

In another well-known instance, King (1970) observed that inflected forms of *be* cannot be contracted if the constituent immediately following them in deep structure appears in some other position elsewhere in the derivation. Thus, *is, am,* and *are* contract freely in (27a–e), but not in (28a-e), where the constituents that followed them are licensed not to be there by VP-deletion, Adverb preposing, WH-Rel movement, Comparative deletion, or WH-Q movement—five different rules.

27a. Sandy's voting for Chris, and I'm voting for her too.

27b. I'm here.

27c. It's that way in real life.

27d. They're very lucky tonight.

27e. The concert's here at 2:00.

28a. Sandy's voting for Chris, and I am/*I'm [ ] too.

28b. Here I am/*I'm [ ].

28c. That's the way it is/*it's [ ] in real life.

28d. They're luckier than we are/*we're [ ] tonight

28e. Tell me where the concert is/*concert's [ ] at 2:00.

In order for Contraction to be stated as a local rule, all five of these movement rules would have to leave a record of their application by inserting some marker when they applied, so that it could be exploited to block the later application of contraction. Similarly global and even transderivational (cf. Lakoff 1972) restrictions are implied in the descriptions of many rules by writers with a wide variety of opinions about the best framework for transformational descriptions.

Lakoff (1970, 1971) argued that the use of such markers was artificial and ad hoc, and that all rules of grammar should be considered to be well-formedness conditions on derivations, or derivational constraints, in the same way that Ross' constraints on variables, Postal's Cross-over principle,[9] and Ross' and Perlmutter's constraints on surface structure are constraints on derivations. Under Lakoff's proposal, for instance, Equi would not be two rules, but a single post-cyclic rule with a cyclic environment, so that the rule involved three phrase markers, summarized as follows:

A pair of phrase markers P_i, P_{i+1} is well formed if

   a. P_{i+1} is identical to P_i except that a certain NP_p in P_i
      is absent in P_{i+1}, and
   b. NP_p and its antecedent in P_i meet certain anaphora
      conditions, and
   c. in that phrase marker P_j which represents the end of the
      cycle on the lowest S containing the antecedent of NP_p,
      NP_p is a subject, and its antecedent meets certain other
      conditions.

Once the theory of global derivational constraints was articulated, many more examples were noticed (e.g., Green 1971, Chomsky 1973: 243), though for some curious reason, many linguists were reluctant to refer to them as global constraints. Along with the examples, a number of questions were raised about the nature and organization of grammatical rules. Constraining the descriptive power of linguistic theories had always been a relevant issue, given the Chomskyan goal of explanatory adequacy, but the proposal of global and transderivational rules made constraining the theory a central concern. Within the Extended Standard Theory (EST), the trace theory of movement rules (Chomsky 1975) was proposed as an alternative to global rules in that it would employ markers of derivational history in a restricted way. It proposed that movement rules left empty NPs (**traces**, abbreviated as *t* or *e*) in the place of moved constituents, so that deletion sites could be referred to by other rules and constraints. Rules of grammar could then refer directly to traces, rather than to a history of movement. The theory of traces was elaborated in several papers by Chomsky and others, e.g., Chomsky (1977, 1981) and Chomsky and Lasnik (1977), and is a cornerstone of the Government and Binding framework.

The EST framework also built on an earlier proposal, which sought to limit the notion 'possible grammar of a natural language' in a different way, by restricting the base component. This is X' (X-Bar) theory, first proposed by

---

[9]Greatly simplified, this principle said that a sentence was ill-formed if its derivation was such that the precedence relations between coreferential NPs in the same clause were not constant (i.e., if a movement rule "crossed an NP over" a coreferential clausemate).

Chomsky (1969), and considerably elaborated by Jackendoff (1977).[10] In this theory, all maximal projections of **major** categories (i.e.: S, NP, VP, AP, PP) have parallel internal constituent structure: they consist of a specifier (Spec) and a head, and their phrasal heads consist of lexical heads and phrasal complements. This is expressed in a template decomposable into two schematic immediate-dominance rules:

$$X'' \rightarrow \text{Spec}, X'$$
$$X' \rightarrow X, \text{(Complements)}$$

where: 1) X ranges over N, V, A, P, S.
          2) X' is defined as the head of X'', and X as the head of X'.
          3) Heads share categorial properties with their mothers.
          4) Complements are X'' categories.

Specifiers include such categories as auxiliary verbs, determiners, and complementizers, the choice in any particular case being a function of the category of the head.

Another proposal which sought to limit the power of descriptive apparatus, and is also incorporated into the EST, is Emonds' (1970/1976) theory of root and structure-preserving rules. Emonds observed that transformational rules were basically **structure-preserving** in that the structures they generated tended to be the same structures that were generated by independently necessary phrase structure rules. He proposed that this was a necessary property of language, and that all rules not belonging to one of two other types must be structure-preserving. The two other types are **root transformations** (rules which apply only to the highest S (or root) in a phrase marker, to conjunct daughters of a coordinate root, or to a direct quotation), and **local transformations** (rules which (a) affect only two constituents which must be strictly adjacent, and (b) are not subject to any conditions exterior to themselves). Subject-Auxiliary Inversion and the constituent question WH-Movement rule were classified as root transformations. Do-support, Quantifier float, and Particle Movement were given as examples of local transformations. Most of the rules that had to be cyclic were claimed to be structure-preserving. Emonds' theory, while providing a strong and transparently motivated restriction on the power of grammars, was criticized on a number of counts (both theoretical and empirical), e.g., by Hooper (1973), Hooper and Thompson (1973), and Green (1976).

In developing the EST, Chomsky increasingly adopted the strategy of postulating that phrase structure rules and transformational rules defined by

---

[10] Jackendoff (1974) provides a convenient introduction.

universal grammar were few in number and extremely general, and supplemented by universal constraints, presumably innate. X-bar theory constrained possible phrase structure rules. It was suggested that a number of general constraints, in addition to the Structure-Preserving Constraint and the A-over-A constraint, limited the set of possible transformations, and these constraints might be **parameterized**, so that they could be specified to differ in subtle ways across languages. For instance, as outlined in Chomsky (1973), the Subjacency Condition prohibited "movement" over more than one NP or S. The Tensed Sentence Condition prohibited extractions from clauses with finite verbs. The Specified Subject Condition prohibited rules from affecting an element following a subject with lexical or non-anaphoric content, in relation to anything outside such a clause. In the theories that have succeeded the EST, these are no longer independent principles, being instead incorporated into clauses in the definition of the theory-specific notions of binding, projection, and proper government.

Relational Grammar, as articulated in public lectures by Postal and Perlmutter in the late 1970s (see now Perlmutter and Postal (1983a); also Johnson and Postal (1980)) also sought to define a restricted theory of universal grammar. It differed from the Standard Theory most conspicuously in its claim that grammatical relations (e.g., subject, direct object, indirect object, oblique object), and not grammatical categories (e.g., NP, Aux), were the primitive elements of syntactic theory, central to the description of the syntax of natural languages, and the basis for a number of substantive constraints on the possible form and syntactic function of syntactic rules. To take just one example, a Relational Succession Law was proposed (Perlmutter and Postal (1983b)) which said that if there is a rule that functions to raise an NP into the next higher clause, that NP will always take on the grammatical relation held by the clause out of which it ascends.

The theoretical innovations described in this section were all proposed as amendments to a single theory which was, in its essentials, about the same as it had been in 1965. The alternative frameworks that exist today under the rubric *generative grammar* differ more radically than these, both from the *Aspects* theory, and from each other.

7 THEORETICAL FRAMEWORKS

In this chapter, we sketch how three influential frameworks for syntactic description compare with their common predecessor, the Standard Theory of the 1960s. We discuss modern phrase structure theories, Chomsky's Government and Binding theory, and the class of theories that have come to be known as Relational Grammar. The first two continue to evolve and mutate at a lively pace, so this chapter aims to provide overviews of current directions in the investigation of syntactic theory, rather than tutorials in specific frameworks.[1] Our discussions focus on levels of syntactic representation, filters, grammatical relations, the treatment of unbounded dependencies and deletions, and the relation between syntactic and semantic representations.

All three of these frameworks evolved from the Standard Theory of transformational grammar during the 1970s. Consequently, while all three share most of the basic assumptions of generative grammar described in Chapter 1, none looks very much like the Standard Theory as described in Chapter 5: a framework with a base component containing a relatively small number of very specific phrase-structure rules, a richly developed transformational component, with a rather larger number of rules, a modest system of filters applying at various levels of representation, and a system of semantic interpretation rules that amounted more to (widely varying) programmatic assumptions than explicit hypotheses. All three frameworks retain the Standard Theory goal of accounting for the fact that language is acquired from fragmentary evidence in a very brief time, and all three take it for granted that a good part of the problem is solved by assuming that an innate universal grammar, common to all languages, has just to be supplemented by a small

---

[1] Sells (1985) provides more detailed descriptions of Government and Binding and Generalized Phrase Structure Grammar. All of theories treated here are the subject of book length expositions (Gazdar, Klein, Pullum, and Sag (1985); Bresnan (1982a); Pollard and Sag (1987, 1994), Borsley and Borjars (2002); Chomsky (1981, 1986b, 1995); Johnson and Postal (1980), Perlmutter (1983), Perlmutter and Rosen (1984), Blake (1990)).

number of language-specific principles and language-specific parameters to universal principles.

7.1 Modern Phrase Structure Theories

As the Extended Standard Theory limited more and more strictly what transformational rules could do, eventually reducing the transformational component to a single rule (see Section 2), investigators (e.g., Gazdar (1981), Kaplan and Bresnan (1982)) began to re-examine the arguments from the 1950s and 1960s that more than one level of syntactic description was necessary to provide an account of the kinds of relations among sentence elements that are found in natural languages. The result was the development of frameworks of generative grammar which provide only a single description of constituent-structure for each structurally unambiguous sentence and which might be called transformationless generative grammar. These include Lexical Functional Grammar (LFG: Kaplan and Bresnan (1982)), Generalized Phrase Structure Grammar (GPSG: Gazdar, Klein, Pullum, and Sag (henceforth GKPS) (1985)) and Head-Driven Phrase Structure Grammar (HPSG: Pollard and Sag (1987, 1994)). When such theories provide separate representations of syntactic and semantic properties of phrases or sentences, each such **level** would only have one description (or **stratum**—cf. Ladusaw (1988)). This contrasts with the Standard Theory, where in addition to multiple levels of representation with different conditions for well-formedness (phonetic, syntactic, semantic), the syntactic level typically had multiple representations (strata) of the same type: namely, the deep structure, the surface structure, and all of the intermediate constituent-structure representations related by the transformations.

Monostratal theories are sometimes referred to as constraint-based or unification-based because the properties of syntactic structures are constrained to be determined by properties of their constituent parts by means of a mathematical operation, similar to set union, called unification (cf. GKPS (1985: 26–27); Pollard and Sag (1987: 27–38)). Modern theories of categorial grammar, which developed from the work of Montague (Montague (1970, 1973)) are also monostratal non-transformational theories. Dowty (1982) and introductory chapters of Moortgat (1988) provide convenient introductions. Some varieties of categorial grammar are unification-based. In general, they are less concerned with constituent structure as an end in itself, than with a transparent account of **semantic compositionality**, a commitment to describing the meaning of every constituent as a function of the meanings of its parts.

GPSG is a highly formalized theory which is integrated with a model-theoretic semantics of the sort described in Dowty, Wall, and Peters (1981).

Categories are defined, like phonemes in generative phonology, as functions from sets of features to their values. Like the Extended Standard Theory, GPSG assumes a version of X-bar theory in the definition of categories (cf. Kornai and Pullum (1990)), but compared to the Standard Theory, the base component is greatly enriched, with an elaboration of the role of syntactic features, and, since there is only one syntactic level, the transformational component is eliminated (Gazdar (1981, 1982); GKPS (1985)). There are universal and language particular restrictions on possible categories in terms of the co-occurrence of various features, but no constraints or filters on derivations, or on deep structure, as there are no derivations, and only one level of structure. The main descriptive mechanisms of a generalized phrase structure grammar are:

- immediate-dominance rules (ID rules), which define what kinds of constituents a category may have as daughters;

- metarules, which induce more ID-rules;

- feature co-occurrence restrictions, which prohibit categories with certain combinations of features

- feature instantiation principles, which constrain values for features of a constituent which are not specified in ID-rules;

- linear precedence rules (LP-rules), which define allowable orders of sister constituents.

With a feature-based definition of category, there are many thousands of categories potentially available for a given grammar, but feature co-occurrence restrictions and feature instantiation principles limit the occurrence of partic-ular feature-value and mother-daughter combinations. An example may serve to show how this works. The ID rule in (1) says that a category with the value "–" for the feature N, "+" for the feature V, 2 for the feature BAR, and "–" for the feature SUBJ (i.e., a verb phrase) can dominate a head daughter of lexical class 2, and an NP daughter.

1. [N–, V+, BAR 2, SUBJ –] → H[SUBCAT 2], [N+, V–, BAR 2]

The Head Feature Convention (HFC) requires the head daughter (identified as "H") to have the same values as its mother for all features in a certain class (and vice versa); this requires the head to be a verb ([N–, V+]), but a feature co-occurrence restriction limits categories which have values for the features N and V and SUBCAT to ones whose value for BAR is 0. Thus, the head daughter's value for BAR is 0, not 2 like its mother's. Consequently, the head daughter is a lexical category, not a phrasal category. Rules like (1) are described as referring to classes of categories because the set consisting of the ordered feature-value pairs {<N, ->, <V, +>, <BAR, 2>, <SUBJ, ->} is a general specification; the rule in (1) licenses equally 3rd singular VPs and 1st plural VPs, with 3rd plural NP daughters and 1st singular NP daughters, etc. The HFC ensures that the person and number specifications on the head daughter will match those for the VP mother.

Since the linear precedence rules hold regardless of category types of mother or daughter, the theory makes the very strong claim of **exhaustive constant partial ordering** (ECPO) for all languages: for all languages, the order of daughters within a constituent is either free, or restricted in the same ways for all constituent types.

Metarules define additional ID rules in terms of other ID rules.[2] For example, passive VPs are defined by means of a passive metarule which says that for every rule which licenses a VP dominating an NP and anything else, there is a corresponding rule in which 1) the VP-node has the value PAS for the feature VFORM (which will license passive morphology), 2) the NP is absent, 3) a *by*-phrase is optionally present, and 4) whatever else might have been specified is specified exactly the same way in the categories defined by the metarule. The HFC ensures that the daughter bears the specification <VFORM, PAS> also.

Thus, a few (universal) feature instantiation principles combine with a small number of (language-particular) metarules and LP-rules and a moderate number of ID rules to define the very large number of well-formed local subtrees needed to describe the structures of sentences in a language.

Unbounded dependency constructions were the basis of the main argument of the 1960s against monostratal grammars; transformations were thought to be indispensable for an account of the fact that a strictly transitive verb might occur without its object at the same time that an apparently extraneous NP showed up somewhere else in the sentence, as in Topicalization or constituent question constructions as illustrated in example (2).

2. The history book, Sandy said Kim put __ in the closet.

In phrase structure theories this is described by licensing the extra NP with an ID rule for clauses and generating in a VP rule what amounts to a trace where the NP would be expected. Naturally, there must be something to guarantee that the extra NP and the trace NP match. This something is the

---

[2]In HPSG, construction types are defined through properties of their lexical heads. Generalizations are expressed through the hierarchical structure of the lexicon, as discussed below.

category-valued feature SLASH in combination with the feature instantiation principles, which have the effect of propagating information about exactly what is absent through relevant nodes of the tree. SLASH is abbreviated "/", and interpreted as 'missing a constituent of the category specified as its value,' so "VP[SLASH NP]" indicates a VP that is missing an NP, either an immediate constituent NP, or one more deeply embedded. SLASH propagation terminates at the lower extreme with a phonologically unrealized constituent as terminal node. Such constituents are represented as categories with a full set of feature specifications, including a value for SLASH that matches their other feature specifications; thus, NP traces have the representation NP[NULL+, α, SLASH[NP α]], where α ranges over sets of feature specifications. Towards the root of the tree, SLASH propagation terminates at the node where the extra or **filler** constituent is licensed. Thus, in addition to the ID rule that corresponds to S → NP VP, there is an ID rule that amounts to S → XP, S/XP; that is, that licenses a sentence that consists of some phrase and a sentence missing a phrase of that type. One of the universal constraints requires that unless the definition of a phrase type specifies otherwise, if any phrasal daughter has a non-empty value for SLASH, the mother will have the same value for SLASH.[3] Thus, information about all features of the absent category are propagated, node by node, up the tree. All of the feature instantiation principles are **local**, which is to say, they constrain the representation of mother and daughters relative to each other, rather than at any greater remove, and every local subtree in a structural representation, and every category in it, must satisfy every constraint in the grammar.

In GPSG, semantic representations in intensional logic[4] are determined **compositionally** (that is,in such a way that the meaning of a constituent is a function of the meanings of its parts), with the semantic type of any phrasal constituent being determinable from its syntactic category, and the semantic types of lexical heads being such that they combine with the types of their complements to give something with the type of the mother.

In GPSG, following a proposal of Dowty (1982), the grammatical relation of a constituent to a verb was treated as being a function of the relative order in which the corresponding argument expression combines semantically with its functor (predicate) expression. Thus, the subject of a predicate expression is the NP whose semantic representation is the last one to combine with the functor it is an argument of, the direct object is the one whose representation

---

[3]Different theories of phrase-structure grammar achieve this effect by different means, but all have essentially this consequence.

[4]The choice of intensional logic is a matter of convenience (GKPS: 9). Nothing in the syntactic theory requires this particular semantic representation.

combines next to last, and the indirect object is the antepenultimate. In LFG, on the other hand, grammatical relations are treated as syntactic primitives which contribute to determining the semantic representations of sentences.

Deletions in transformational grammar do not in general correspond to phonologically null categories in monostratal theories. The treatment of infinitive complements for verbs like *try, persuade* and *seem*, for example, involves just generating complement VPs rather than complement Ss, and indicating that the complement VP is interpreted as having the same subject as the VP it is part of.

HPSG (Pollard and Sag (1987, 1994)) receives its name from the role played by the projection of information from the lexical heads of phrases. It is similar to GPSG in being constraint-based, and formalized in terms of feature structures. It retains several of the descriptive mechanisms and principles of GPSG (e.g., the ID/LP distinction). It provides an increased role for the lexicon and the semantics, and a diminished role for ID rules. Constituent structure is determined by subcategorization information in a hierarchially structured lexicon (cf. Davis and Koenig 2000) in conjunction with the set of hierarchical phrase-type definitions (or ID-schemata, in some versions), which may be partly language-specific.

Feature structures in HPSG are constrained by being defined as terms in an ontology of types, each defined in terms of what attributes (features) it has, and what the type of the value of each feature is. The types form a **multiple inheritance** hierarchy. Being in an inheritance hierarchy means that subtypes have all of the properties of all of their supertypes, unless one of their specified feature-values overrides a value specified as a default value in the definition of the supertype (inheritance), and they never have values for any feature which are inconsistent with non-default values their supertypes have. The hierarchies are multiple inheritance hierarchies because relevant classifications of words and phrases cross-cut each other. Thus, a VP is a third person singular ditransitive VP because of its position in separate agreement and argument-structure hierarchies. Together, the type definitions and the type hierarchy do the work done in GPSG by feature co-occurrence restrictions, ID-rules, and metarules to constrain possible categories or constituent types.

Grammatical relations in HPSG are represented in terms of the obliqueness hierarchy described by Keenan and Comrie (1977): the list of categories that constitutes a description of a lexical item's required arguments is ordered by obliqueness, with subject being the least oblique relation, direct object being the next least oblique, etc. In general, this analysis identifies constituents as having the same grammatical relation as GPSG and LFG (and Relational Grammar) accounts do, but by different means.

The most striking differences between HPSG and GPSG stem from the expanded use in HPSG of unification (and structure-sharing); not only universal principles of various sorts, but also lexical representations of particular words require that the value for some feature in the representation unify with the value for some other feature. The treatments of controlled VPs and unbounded dependency constructions differ more in implementation than in spirit. More detailed introductions to HPSG can be found in Sag and Wasow (1999), and Green (2002).

7.2 The Government and Binding Theory

Government and Binding (GB) is a transformational theory with several distinct levels of representation, as represented in (3): transformations define multiple strata relating a syntactic level of S-structure to D-structure (which corresponds closely to the Standard Theory's Deep Structure) and to a level of Logical Form, where certain logical relations are represented.

3.

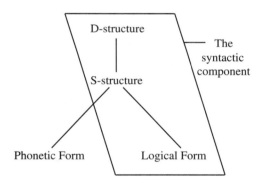

The level of Phonetic Form, which roughly corresponds to Standard Theory Surface Structure, is not considered to be a syntactic level. The rules relating S-structure to Phonetic Form apply to syntactic units, but do not conform to the principles that constrain other components of the syntax. Two proposals which contributed to the evolution of the Extended Standard Theory and GB, the X-bar proposal of parallel category structure, and the Structure-Preserving Constraint, were described in Chapter 6. Compared to the Standard Theory, GB greatly reduces the transformational component and expands the role of filtering principles and distinct levels of representation. Representations at each level are further constrained by GB's Projection Principle, which requires that representations at every syntactic level observe the subcategorization requirements of lexical items.

The transformational component is reduced to a single major[5] rule, Move-α, where α is a variable ranging over constituent types. Thus, the rule (unfortunately framed as an imperative) amounts to: constituents can appear in a position where they are not directly licensed by constituent-structure constraints (X-bar schemata). The transformational rule does not specify what sort of constituent may appear in what sort of site under what conditions. The work of constraining relations between D-Structure, S-Structure, and LF positions is effected by a system of filters and global constraints, called principles. Move-α applies cyclically to structural representations to define S-structures and logical forms. Each instance of Move-α defines a phrase-marker with a coindexed trace indicating the position of the constituent in the preceding phrase-marker, so that its path can be traced like a path of footsteps, as in (4).

4.

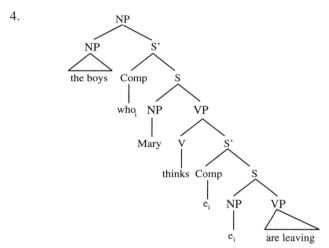

Stylistic movement rules, deletion rules, filters and phonological rules map S-structures into Phonetic Form. Other rules, including Quantifier Raising (as an instance of Move-α) and various interpretive rules map S-structure into Logical Form.

Grammatical relations are defined configurationally, as in the Standard Theory (with some extensions and elaborations (Chomsky (1981: 209ff)): subjects are NPs which are sisters of a VP, and are dominated directly by S, and so on. **Thematic roles** such as agent, patient and goal (cf. Gruber (1965), Jackendoff (1972)) are not linked directly to grammatical relations. The Theta Criterion (θ-Criterion) of GB stipulates that each argument bears

---

[5]There may also be minor local rules of the sort defined by Emonds (1970/1976) (cf. Borer 1981).

one and only one thematic role (θ-role), and each thematic role is assigned to one and only one argument. The Projection Principle is extended (as the Extended Projection Principle, or EPP) to apply to thematic roles so that the Theta Criterion holds not only at D-Structure, but at all levels. It follows from this that rules cannot have the effect of changing thematic relations.

There are no deletion relations in the syntactic component of GB, since Move-α does not define deletions. The effect of deletion under identity is achieved by freely licensing empty NPs and then filtering out trees which do not conform to the Empty Category Principle (ECP) and binding principles. The ECP has the effect of requiring an empty NP to either be a sister of a lexical category (N, V, A, or P), or to have a coindexed non-argument antecedent within a specified local domain. These two conditions define the notion **proper government**. Binding principles apply to freely indexed NPs, including base-generated empty NPs, and to traces licensed by Move-α, which are coindexed with the moved NP. The conditions of the Binding Theory require reflexive pronouns to have coindexed antecedents (and definite pronouns not to have antecedents) in their governing category. Pollard and Sag (1994) (Chapter 6) sketches some problems with the GB binding theory.

In the Standard Theory, many rules had to apply cyclically, but cyclicity had to be stipulated for each such rule, since not all rules could be successive-cyclic. In GB, the principle of Subjacency (Chomsky (1973, 1981)) stipulates that there are no unbounded movements, and requires that apparently un-bounded movements be accomplished via successive cyclic application, one bounding node (clause or NP) at a time. In effect, this makes all applications of Move-α successive-cyclic. The effect of unboundedness is achieved by allowing Move-α to move an NP to COMP(lementizer) position, and from there (successively) to the next higher COMP, indefinitely (subject to other principles of the grammar, of course).

As is probably evident, filters play a central role in GB: in addition to the filtering functions of the Projection Principle, the principle of Subjacency, the Binding Principles, and the Empty Category Principle, there is a Case Filter which requires non-empty NPs to be assigned an abstract case by language-specific abstract-case assignment principles. In the GB account, one of the characteristics of passive verbs is that they fail to assign case to their objects. Consequently, the Case Filter requires that the objects move to subject position, where they can be assigned a case by the inflection constituent (INFL). Abstract cases are expressly described as not necessarily corresponding to morphological cases.

The Barriers theory (Chomsky 1986b) was designed to refine the notion of locality needed to constrain so-called "unbounded" extraction dependencies, and relate it to the notion of locality invoked in accounts of case-marking and binding.

In the Minimalist Program (Chomsky 1995), the number of distinguished levels is reduced to two (PF and LF), driven by the goal of deriving syntactic constraints from functional requirements of of the semantics and considerations of phonology, and constraints apply either at one of the levels, or at all strata in a derivation. As a consequence of these "economy conditions," constituents do not "move" freely, but only to satisfy a constraint. The X-bar theory and government are no longer essential to the theory. In early versions of minimalism, transderivational constraints (looked at askance in the 1970s) play a crucial role: derivation were more highly valued to the extent that they minimize structure and the length of derivations, which of course can only be determined by comparing derivations and grammars.

7.3   Relational Grammar (RG)

Relational Grammar (RG) is similar to the Standard Theory in assuming syntactic derivations of multiple strata at a single level of representation, but diverges in taking grammatical relations (such as subject, direct object, indirect object) as primitives in syntactic representations, rather than defining grammatical relations derivatively, as the Standard Theory does in terms of phrase structure, or as GPSG and categorial grammar do in terms of their semantic relations. In RG, rules relating adjacent strata are stated directly in terms of grammatical relations. RG recognizes such **term** relations as subject-of (abbreviated as "1"), direct object-of ("2"), indirect object-of ("3"), and such **oblique** relations as Locative, Directional, Benefactive, Instrumental, as well as **overlay** grammatical relations like Q′ (for question element), Rel′ (for relative pronoun), Top (for topicalized element, and OW (for overweight, i.e., bearing an extraordinary semantic or phonetic load). In addition, there are named grammatical relations for elements that used to bear a specified term grammatical relation which some other element has come to bear. These are the **chômeur** relations, and the **emeritus** relation (found in clause union constructions such as causatives). The name *chômeur* means 'unemployed' in French, and is used to describe the grammatical relation of an element that used to have a certain term grammatical relation to some other element. Thus there are 1-chômeurs, 2-chômeurs, and 3-chômeurs (written as $\hat{1}$, $\hat{2}$ etc., with the circumflex accent from *chômeur*, or just as Cho), corresponding to constituents that were subjects, direct objects, etc. in a preceding stratum.

RG is characterized by the following claims:

1) Grammatical relations are primitive notions, not defined in terms of any others.

2) Grammatical relations are related to each other in a universal hierarchy with subjects highest, followed by direct objects, indirect objects, and more oblique objects, in that order. The hierarchy is universal.

3) Grammatical relations figure directly in syntactic representations.

The grammatical relation holding between two elements is represented as an arc connecting them, and labelled with the relation (e.g., p (for 'predicate'), 1 (subject) etc.) and the stratum, as in the relational network (5a) and the equivalent stratal diagram (5b).

(5a)   (5b)

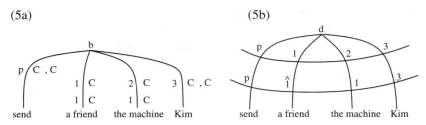

The two chief motivations in the genesis of RG were (a) (in common with other generative theories) the desire to make cross-linguistic generalizations about grammatical phenomena, and (b) the need to refer directly to grammatical relations in describing language-internal grammatical phenomena (Postal (1976)). Thus, one of the developments which prepared the way for relational grammar was the observation that some rules seemed to refer crucially to such notions as subject and direct object. For example, Equi-NP-deletion (6a,b) was most perspicuously described as deleting the subject of a complement clause, Raising (6c,d) as making the subject of a complement clause the object of a transitive embedding verb, or the subject of an intransitive embedding verb. Heavy NP Shift (6e) and Tough-movement (6f) were most perspicuously described as affecting non-subjects.[6]

6a. Kim is eager [ ] to please Sandy.
6b. Kim persuaded Sandy [ ] to leave.
6c. Kim expects Sandy [ ] to have passed the test.
6d. Sandy seems [ ] to have won the match.
6e. They attributed [ ] to arson the blaze which destroyed half a block of downtown Champaign.
6f. Sandy is easy for Kim to please [ ].

---

[6]See Postal (1974) for a relatively complete discussion of the relevant issues.

To some extent it was possible to formulate such rules within the linear and structural constraints imposed by the Standard Theory (cf. Berman 1974a), but the results were often unwieldy, and required arbitrary decisions which had unwelcome repercussions elsewhere in the grammar.

The other relevant development was the growing interest in **substantive universals** (universal properties of languages which are not a consequence of the assumptions in which they are framed (cf. Chomsky (1965))), and in accounts for the fact that many languages seem to have rules which it is natural to identify with intuitively similar rules of other languages, even though they have no morphological or formal similarities when stated in terms provided by the Standard Theory. For example, many languages seem to have a rule that it is natural to call The Passive, although the structural similarity to a transformational rule for English passive constructions, when stated in the Standard Theory notation, as in (7), may be slight or non-existent.

7.		X	–	NP	–	V	–	NP	–	Y
	SD:	1		2		3		4		5
	SC:	1		4		be 3+en		by 2		5

Word order might not be affected at all, and of course, the morphology of the verb and the marking of the ex-subject would be different. The Standard Theory made no distinction in importance between the relative positions of the NPs referred to by the indices 2 and 4, and the presence of *be*, *-en*, and *by*. But if the English passive rule was stated in relational terms, as in (8a) or (8b), as promoting an object NP to subject status, then in accordance with a principle described below (the Chômeur Law), which demoted the original subject to a sort of relational limbo where it took on the markings of an oblique object, it was easy to see the passive rules in diverse languages as identical, except for morphological form, and one expected morphological form to be determined by language-particular rules.

8a. Direct object → subject

8b. 2 → 1

The number of strata that a basic clause[7] might have is limited by the number of grammatical relations, the number of constituents in the clause, the number of rules affecting grammatical relations, and the principles (or laws) limiting their interaction which form the heart of RG theory.

---

[7]A basic clause is somewhat like a kernel sentence in the *Syntactic Structures* theory, in that nonbasic clauses are composed of combinations of them, and every surface clause entails the existence of at least one of them.

Grammatical relations are relations of an argument expression to a lexical predicate, and rules that change grammatical relations are all either clause-bound or affect at most two adjacent clauses. Indeed, one of the initial observations of RG was that relation-changing rules tended to correspond to those rules in transformational grammar that had to apply cyclically.

The RG analyses of various languages involve a relatively small number of rules, and differ mainly in which lexical items trigger which rules, partly because a large number of substantive constraints (referred to as laws of universal grammar) limit the set of possible relation-changing rules. A number of such laws have been articulated in RG and Arc-Pair Grammar (APG) (Johnson and Postal (1980)). A few will be described here. The Relational Succession Law (Perlmutter and Postal (1983b: 53ff)) says that an NP which ascends into a higher clause assumes the grammatical relation borne by the clause out of which it ascends. The Oblique Law (Perlmutter and Postal (1983a: 90)) requires that if a nominal bears some oblique relation in some stratum in a clause, then it bears that relation in the initial stratum as well. In other words, once an oblique, always previously an oblique. This means that there can be no rules demoting terms (such as subjects) to obliques (like instrument), or making chômeurs into obliques, or changing one oblique relation to another.

The Stratal Uniqueness Law (Perlmutter and Postal (1983a: 92)) says that no stratum can contain more than one term arc for each term relation, i.e., no more than one 1-arc, one 2-arc, or one 3-arc, and the Chômeur Law (Perlmutter and Postal (1983a: 96)) defines what happens when the state required by the Stratal Uniqueness Law is threatened. It says that if a nominal N_a bears some term relation in a stratum C_i, and a nominal N_b bears that relation in stratum C_{i+1}, then N_a is a chômeur in C_{i+1}. The Motivated Chômage Law (Perlmutter and Postal (1983a: 99)) says that chômeurs only exist under the condition just described. This is one of the more controversial claims of RG. It has been challenged by (among others) Keenan (1975) and Comrie (1977), and defended by Perlmutter (1978) and Perlmutter and Postal (1984a,b).

The Nuclear Dummy Law (Perlmutter and Postal (1983a: 103)) states that if A is an arc whose head is a dummy nominal, A is a nuclear term arc. That is, dummies like extraposition *it*, and *there*-insertion *there* can only be subjects or objects. This entails that they cannot be indirect objects, obliques, chômeurs, topics, or anything else.

The work of Keenan and Comrie (1977) showing the relevance of grammatical relations for relativization strategies[8] figured significantly at first in

---

[8] Keenan and Comrie (1977) gave evidence for a hierarchy, described in terms of grammatical relations, of accessibility of NPs in a clause to be relativized (i.e., to represent the gap or NP

attracting attention to RG, but unbounded dependency constructions have not been the focus of much research or discussion in RG since then. As of this writing, RG has had little to say about what constrains the relations between fillers and gaps in unbounded dependency constructions, although the topic is addressed in Johnson and Postal (1980).

In the early days of relational grammar, deletion phenomena such as Equi-NP-deletion were treated as syntactic deletions under identity, as in the Standard Theory. More recently, the fact that some term is understood as simultaneously bearing grammatical relations to two (or more) different predicates is represented by allowing a single term to head more than one arc (multidomination); arcs with different labels connect that term to the verbs to which it bears grammatical relations. In this respect, RG is more similar to constraint-based theories than to derivational ones.

7.4 Perspective

This chapter does not exhaust the stock of distinct grammatical theories currently being explored, though it has tried to sketch those in which the most influential research has been published. To be sure, the composition of the set so characterized may change in three years' time; it is a truism to say that grammatical theory is in flux. It has been since the 1950s, and would probably be boring and cease to inspire research if it were not.

There is, of course, a healthy competition among the various frameworks, but it is encouraging to note the almost complete absence of excessive polemic which characterized the theoretical divisions in the early 1970s. Linguists working in a particular framework are paying more attention to the results being derived in other frameworks, and are concerned that their own should be able to give a natural, principled account of the valid generalizations that the others uncover.

---

coreferential to the head of the relative clause). The hierarchy was such that subjects relativize most easily, then direct objects, then indirect objects, then oblique objects, then genitive NPs, then objects of comparison. Thus, a language might relativize only subjects, or only subjects and direct objects, but never only direct objects, or only subjects and indirect objects, and so on.

APPENDIX: REFERENCE GUIDE TO SYNTACTIC DESCRIPTION

Introduction

The phenomena described in this appendix cover most of the structures discussed in the transformational literature. They are identified by the names of the rules that traditionally described them in the generative grammar literature. Most of these constructions have counterparts in other languages.

It is a good idea to cultivate an acquaintance with these rules, since familiarity with the older descriptions which they represent is assumed in much current technical literature, even in frameworks that do not use transformational principles. Current generative theories tend to have a minimum of transformations, if they have any at all. In such theories, the work done by transformational rules in older theories is distributed among various non-transformational principles. But even in such theories, the constructions associated with transformations continue to be important phenomena, and they are often referred to by the traditional names of the transformational rules.

Much of the description in this appendix is oversimplified. No arguments are presented that the phenomena discussed under a given rubric must be the effects of a single rule or constraint, and many of the known complications and conditions are not mentioned. But the phenomena described by these rules are familiar in some form or another to most generative grammarians, and if the descriptions contained herein are not entirely accurate, they should at least serve to guide further research.

The references we give for each construction or phenomenon are meant to be suggestive, not exhaustive, though an effort has been made to include the primary sources, the articles or books where the various constructions were first discussed within the transformational framework. Berman and Schmerling (1973), Gazdar, Pullum, and Klein (1978), and Smith and Johnsen (1981) may provide more complete bibliography, within their limits. In addition, Quirk, Greenbaum, Leech, and Svartvik (1972) provides a wealth of relevant and accessible information on a wide variety of English constructions.

Since our goal is to provide a clear but informal description of each construction, we have not adopted the conventional transformational formalism. Since the use of that formalism amounts to describing structures entirely in terms of strings, it is at once too vague, and too restrictive.[1] To illustrate, there are several ways one might describe the construction associated with the rule of Equi-NP-deletion. The rule of Equi-NP-Deletion would have been described formally (with ad hoc modifications, and nonetheless still incompletely or inaccurately specified)[2] more or less[3] as in (1), where the top line represents the structural analysis of a constituent structure (see Sec. 5.2), the second line indexes the analysis, and the third line specifies differences that the rule defines.

(1) Formal description:
    Equi-NP-Deletion:

	X	NP	AUX	V	(NP)	Y	NP	AUX	Z
SD:	1	2	3	4	5	6	7	8	9
SC:	1	2	3	4	5	6	0	8	9

    Conditions: 7 is identical to 2 or 5
                       4 governs Equi

Several properties of this description are worth remarking on. First, the list of conditions in (1) is already an ad hoc patch on a system not designed to describe what practitioners wanted it to describe (see Perlmutter 1971:123–134).

---

[1] It is too vague in that without ad hoc annotations it does not allow one to specify unambiguously all relevant structural properties in a structural analysis, and sometimes there are multiple possibilities. In addition, it does not allow unambiguous specification of transformational operations. Linguists once supposed that they would soon infer universal properties from which such details would follow, but it never happened. The conventional formalism is too restrictive in that it allows reference only to syntactic categories and variables, to the exclusion of, e.g., clause boundaries, grammatical relations (like subject), and case (like non-nominative). See Borkin (1971), Akmajian and Heny (1975), McCawley (1978a) for further discussion. Some current research continues to assume that no such details need to be mentioned since they will follow as consequences of universal constraints, but in most cases, adequate constraints of this sort remain to be worked out.

We have not described the constructions in the informal shorthand prose of transformational grammar either, because of the pernicious metaphors (described in Chapter 1) that are its backbone. But in order to make this appendix as useful as possible, we have also eschewed descriptions in terms of well-formedness conditions on derivations, even though we believe that they are the least misleading. Instead, we have tried to describe phenomena or constructions in the most theory-neutral terms possible, occasionally describing them in terms of how relevant structures differ from canonical forms.

[2] Whether incompletely or inaccurately depends on what set of conventions is adopted for interpreting the formal representation. Since all of the conventions were themselves incomplete and only partially empirically defensible, we do not elaborate.

[3] Whether more or less depends on the set of base rules, transformations, and constraints adopted. A change in any one could easily affect the empirical correctness of the rule.

Second, the nature of the identity required was not specified. Early work (e.g., McCawley 1971b, Morgan 1970) argued that it was not just identity of form. This conclusion rested on the assumption that presupposed coreference (see Postal 1970) was a syntactic property which required representation as referential indices. It is now generally agreed that the relevant kind of identity is a **pragmatic** property (the property of being intended to indicate the same referent), which may affect the usability of sentences in particular contexts, but perhaps not their grammaticality (see Green 1981).

Third, whether constituent 7 had to be identical to 2 or to 5 was supposed to depend on the structure (cf. Rosenbaum's (1967) Minimal Distance Principle) or on the verb.

Fourth, describing the sensitivity of this deletion to the presence of certain verbs by saying "4 governs Equi" is (obviously) not very helpful, but no less so than any of the other ways prompted by this notation, e.g., "4 is a member of the governing class", "4 is marked [+Equi]". These formulations might look more elegant, but they are in fact no more explicit. Listing the verbs would be more explicit, but if anything, less elegant.

Equi-NP-Deletion might have been characterized informally as in (2).

(2) Informal Description:

> Equi-NP-Deletion deletes the subject NP of a complement clause if the NP is identical to an NP in the embedding sentence, and the main verb of the embedding S is a member of the governing class, which includes such verbs as *want, hope, expect, persuade,* and *promise.*

(Actually, the conventional formalism does not allow direct reference to grammatical relations such as "subject of"; cf. Postal 1976 for discussion.) Equi-NP-deletion ought to have been described as something like (3), but is characterized informally here as in (4).

(3) Less misleading explicit description:

> In a derivation $<PM_0, ..., PM_n>$ (where PM_0 is a deep structure, and PM_n is a surface structure) containing a PM_i such that the subject NP_k of some complement clause is identical to some NP in the next higher clause, and the verb of the next higher clause is of a certain class (including *want, hope, expect,* and others), then the pair of adjacent phrase-markers $<PM_i, PM_{i+1}>$ is well-formed if PM_i is as just described and PM_{i+1} is identical except that the node corresponding to the subject NP_k is absent.

(4) Informal characterization adopted here:

> A subject NP in a complement clause may be absent provided that the main verb in the embedding S is a member of the governing class, which includes verbs like *try, want, hope, expect,* etc. The complement clause will be understood as if it had a subject NP bound by (i.e., coreferential with) a NP in the embedding clause.

Identifying the contructions described here in terms of the transformational rules once supposed to describe them is intended to make references to the older literature comprehensible without requiring detailed knowledge of the theory in which those references were framed.

Other informal, but hopefully not misleading, characterizations have such forms as:

> This rule relates structures of a certain form to structures identical except that ...
> The verb is marked to agree in number and person with its subject.

This last form is shorthand for:

> This rule relates structures in which the verb is not marked for agreement (or is marked, but doesn't agree with its subject), and structures in which the verb is marked to agree in number and person with its subject.

The description of each rule or construction includes an illustration, consisting of a schematic representation (in capital letters) of an example that meets the structural description of the rule (the 'input' to the rule, in that unfortunate metaphor) connected by a double-headed arrow to a string of symbols that exemplifies the structural change of the rule (the 'output' of the rule). We use double-headed arrows ($\longleftrightarrow$) rather than right-headed arrows, to remind the reader of the non-directionality of derivations. The X-arrow ($\leftarrow$X$\rightarrow$) is used in illustrations to indicate that the two structures are **not** related by the rule in question.

Conventions and Definitions

In the examples below and elsewhere, lower-case alphabetic SUBSCRIPTS are used to indicate sameness of intended or understood reference.

RULE GOVERNMENT. A rule or phenomenon is said to be **governed** if it is limited to an environment linked to certain lexical items–usually a subset of a certain category (most often Verb). The set is frequently definable only in semantic or pragmatic terms. For instance, a rule which applied to the complements of certain verbs, but not to the complements of other verbs, would be governed.

References: G. Lakoff 1965, R. Lakoff 1968, Green and Morgan 1976, Green 1981.

OPTIONAL and OBLIGATORY. These terms are used to specify a certain kind of non-structural condition on a transformation. An **optional** transformation requires that in a derivation containing a phrase-marker PM_i that meets the structural description of the transformation, the adjacent phrase-marker PM_{i+1} may have the properties specified in the structural change of the rule. An **obligatory** transformation, on the other hand, requires that PM_{i+k} ($k \geq$ 1) (i.e., some phrase-marker later in the derivation) must have the properties specified in the structural change.

COMMAND. The original definition of this term stipulates that a node A **commands** a node B if the closest S node dominating A also dominates B, provided that neither A nor B dominates the other. In the tree below,

A commands B, C, D, S_3, E, and F, but not S_2, G, H, I, or J.
B commands A, S_2, G, H, I, and J, but not C, D, S_3, E, or F.
G commands H, I, and J, and nothing else.
C commands D, S_3, E, and F, as well as A and everything A dominates, but not B.

And so on.

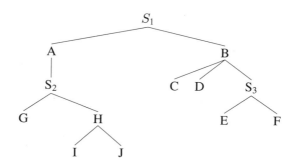

In more recent work, the notion of 'command' has been generalized (as **C-command** or **M-command**) by substituting "branching node" or "maximal projection" (i.e., NP, VP, PP, AP or S') for S in the original definition.

References: Langacker 1966, Ross 1967/83, Reinhart 1983.

VARIABLE. Some transformations (including the one in (1)) were formulated with **variables** (by convention, upper-case letters from the end of the Latin alphabet) in their structural description. In some cases the variables are merely for expository convenience, in that the variable could be replaced by a finite list of categories (or of finite sequences of categories) that could occur in the position of the variable. Such variables are sometimes called **abbreviatory variables**. In other cases, the variable is used to represent the fact that a dependency between two elements involved is **unbounded**, that is, can be an arbitrarily long sequence of categories. In such cases, the rule cannot be formulated at all without a variable; such variables are called **essential variables**.

ASTERISK: An asterisk ('*') marks a following expression as ungrammatical. Beware: some writers use the asterisk to indicate unacceptability without taking a position on whether the item so stigmatized should be treated as ungrammatical.

Other stigmata: The percent sign ('%') prefixes a form about whose acceptability or grammaticality dialects differ. The exclamation point ('!') indicates that the expression reflects very unusual presuppositions. In some works, an ampersand ('&') is used to indicate that a sentence is ambiguous in a relevant way.

Single-Clause Phenomena

NP Movement Constructions

1. Passive. Optional, governed.

Active transitive clauses have passive counterparts where the passive form differs from the active in that

(a) the subject of the active clause is the object of *by* in a PP that follows the verb.

(b) the direct object phrase is the subject.

(c) the verb *be* precedes the verb.

(d) the active verb is in its past participle form.

Chris SAW LOU ⟷ Lou was seen by Chris.

Chris GAVE A BOOK TO LOU ⟷ A book was given by Chris to Lou.

Chris GAVE LOU A BOOK ⟷ Lou was given a book by Chris.

LOU HAS A HAMMER ←X→ *A hammer is had by Lou.

MANY PEOPLE BELIEVE THAT CHRIS IS A DEAN ⟷
That Chris is a dean is believed by many people.

MOST PEOPLE BELIEVE CHRIS TO BE A DEAN ⟷
Chris is believed to be a dean by most people.

This rule is governed, licensing passives with *take*, for example, but not *cost*. It is obligatory for a very few verbs, including *rumor*. In the GB tradition, passive is a key example of A-Movement (movement to argument position).

References and complications: R. Lakoff 1971, Siegel 1973, Chomsky 1973, Johnson 1974, Green and Morgan 1976, Perlmutter and Postal 1977, Davison 1980, Green forthcoming.

2. Heavy NP Shift. Optional, ungoverned.

If a sentence contains a sufficiently long or contextually significant object NP, that NP may occur at the end of its clause, after more oblique complements.

THEY ATTRIBUTED THE FIRE THAT STARTED LAST NIGHT IN THE BARN ACROSS THE ROAD TO ARSON ⟷
They attributed to arson the fire that started last night in the barn across the road.

Short, simple NPs and subject NPs do not have this privilege of occurrence:

I ATTRIBUTED THE FIRE TO ARSON ←X→
*I attributed to arson the fire.

THE FIRE THAT STARTED LAST NIGHT IN THE BARN ACROSS THE ROAD WAS ATTRIBUTED TO ARSON ←X→
*Was attributed to arson the fire that started last night in the barn across the road.

The construction is upper-bounded, that is, the "shifted" NP never occurs any farther from its normal position than the end of its own clause.

THAT I DISTRIBUTED PICTURE POSTCARDS MADE BY JOHN J. JINGLEHEIMER-SMITH TO THEM WAS NOT PUBLICIZED
⟶ That I distributed to them picture postcards made by John J. Jingleheimer-Smith was not publicized.
←X→ *That I distributed to them was not publicized picture postcards made by John J. Jingleheimer-Smith.

Subjects which follow an auxiliary may not be shifted, but logical subjects in object position may:

ARE JOHN J. JINGLEHEIMER-SMITH AND HIS FAITHFUL DOG SANDY PRESENT
←X→ *Are present John J. Jingleheimer-Smith and his faithful dog Sandy?

THEY BELIEVE JOHN J. JINGLEHEIMER-SMITH AND HIS FAITHFUL DOG SANDY TO BE PRESENT ⟷
They believe to be present John J. Jingleheimer-Smith and his faithful dog Sandy.

As seen in these examples, "heaviness" is not strictly a function of syntactic structure or either relative or absolute phonological substance; a very long personal name counts as "heavy," and as Postal 1974 shows, a single quantifier suffices to make an NP heavy enough to be clause-final.

And he put in charge of the CIA George Herbert Walker Bush.

Harry gave to Hermione the entire sheaf.

This phenomenon occurs in many languages, often with different restrictions than in English.

References and complications: Postal 1974.

Other Reordering Constructions

3. Particle movement. Usually optional, governed to the extent that it does not apply to some verb-particle combinations when the object is a non-pronominal NP.

Given a transitive predicate consisting of a verb and a preposition (called a **particle** in these constructions to distinguish it from other uses of the preposition) the direct object NP may appear before the particle.

DALE LOOKED UP THE NUMBER $\longleftrightarrow$ Dale looked the number up.

Transitive particle-verbs are distinguished from Verb + Prepositional Phrase sequences by the fact that 1) true prepositions cannot immediately follow their objects, and 2) particles may not be Pied Piped (i.e., may not appear at the front of sentences with the NP when the object is the focus of a question or relative clause). Thus:

DALE TURNED OFF THE LIGHT $\longleftrightarrow$ Dale turned the light off.

DALE TURNED OFF THE EXPRESSWAY $\leftarrow$X$\rightarrow$
*Dale turned the expressway off.

Dale sat in a chair.   (Preposition)
In what did Dale sit?

Dale phoned in an order.   (Particle)
*In what did Dale phone?

If the NP is an unstressed pronoun, it must not follow the unshifted particle.

*I looked up him   (Cf.: I looked him up.)
*I put away it   (Cf.: I put it away.)

Some particle verbs, e.g., *pull off* (= 'carry out, do') appear to permit the particle to follow the NP objects ONLY when the object is a pronoun, i.e., when being in that position is in fact required.

THE GENERALS PULLED OFF A COUP ←X→
*The generals pulled a coup off.

THEY PULLED OFF IT ⟷ They pulled it off.

There may be other verb-particle combinations which never allow the particle to appear separated from the verb. The particle construction is one of the few constructions in this compilation which is more or less specific to English, though there are some obvious correspondences to German "separable prefix" verbs.

References and complications: Fraser 1973, Jacobson 1987, Ojeda 1987, Sadock 1987.

4. Affix hopping. Ungoverned, obligatory.

In the *Syntactic Structures* and *Aspects* versions of transformational grammar, an Aux(iliary) constituent optionally dominated nodes labelled Modal (dominating the formatives *will, may, can, shall, must*), Perf, and Prog (dominating *have -en*, and *be -ing*, respectively) in that order. It obligatorily dominated a node labelled Tense, ultimately dominating either a present or a past tense formative before any of these. All of this was accomplished by a phrase structure rule along the lines of:

Aux ⟶ Tense (Modal) (Perf) (Prog)

This meant that a transformation, known in the standard theory as Affix Hopping, or Affix Shift, (and in the Government-Binding framework as rule R, head movement, or verb movement) was necessary to guarantee that the affixes were correctly attached in surface structure. The rule was usually formulated something like this:

$$X - \left\{ \begin{array}{c} \text{Tense} \\ \text{-en} \\ \text{-ing} \end{array} \right\} - \left\{ \begin{array}{c} V \\ \text{Modal} \\ \text{have} \\ \text{be} \end{array} \right\} - Y$$

1	2	3	4	⟹
1	0	3+2	4	

The rule has the ad hoc appearance it has because the analysis it presupposes does not make Tense, -en, and -ing, or V, Modal, *have,* and *be* members of the same category. What it says is that some tree in which a member of the set {Tense,-*en,* -*ing*} (known by the ad hoc name "affix") precedes a member of the set {V, Modal, *have, be*} ("verbal elements") must be adjacent in a derivation to a phrase-marker which is identical except that each affix is a right sister of the verbal element that followed it.

KIM pres HAVE -EN WRITE A LETTER ⟷
Kim have+pres write+en a letter.

KIM pres MAY HAVE BE -ING WATCH TV ⟷
Kim may+pres have be+en watch+ing TV.

References and complications: Chomsky 1957, 1965; Ross 1969d, McCawley 1971a, Pullum and Wilson 1977, Gazdar, Pullum and Sag 1982, Koopman 1984, Pollock 1989.

5. Adjective preposing. Usually obligatory, governed.
     An NP consisting of an NP and an adjective phrase may appear in an adjacent phrase-marker with the adjective head of the adjective phrase preceding the noun head of the NP.

[THE MAN WHO IS TALLEST WILL WIN ⟶]
THE MAN TALLEST WILL WIN ⟷
The tallest man will win.

[THE MAN WHO IS EASIEST TO PLEASE IS CHRIS ⟶]
THE MAN EASIEST TO PLEASE IS CHRIS ⟷
The easiest man to please is Chris.

If the NP is headed by an indefinite pronoun like *someone, no one, everybody,* or interrogative *who,* rather than a noun, the adjective cannot precede it.

SOMEONE UNKNOWN COULD WIN ←X→
*Unknown someone could win.
WHO SMARTER THAN THAT WOULD RUN ←X→
*Smarter who than that would run?

Passive and progressive participles may occur either before a head noun or after it, if they have no complements or adjuncts:

THE MAN WHO WAS MURDERED WAS FROM BEAN BLOSSOM, INDIANA ←...→
The murdered man was from Bean Blossom, Indiana.

THE KITTEN WHICH IS SLEEPING IS FOR YOU ←...→
The sleeping kitten is for you.

Compare:

*The sleeping kitten since 9:00
*The nominated man by Terry

Adjectives derived from appositive (non-restrictive) as well as restrictive relative clauses are preposable:

THE UNDERGRADUATES WHO ARE INDUSTRIOUS WILL OUT-PERFORM THE LAZY ONES
←...→ The industrious undergraduates will outperform the lazy ones.

THE UNDERGRADUATES, WHO ARE INDUSTRIOUS, WILL OUT-PERFORM THE ALUMNI
←...→ The industrious undergraduates will outperform the alumni.

This construction is lexically governed in that, for most speakers, certain adjectives (for example, *afraid*, *content*, and *ill*) do not occur before the noun.

DELBERT IS THE BOY WHO IS SCARED ←...→
Delbert is the scared boy.

DELBERT IS THE BOY WHO IS AFRAID ←...X→
*Delbert is the afraid boy.

A MAN WHO IS CONTENTED IS HARD TO FIND ←...→
A contented man is hard to find.

A MAN WHO IS CONTENT IS HARD TO FIND ←...X→
*A content man is hard to find.

Versions of this construction are found in a variety of languages. The restrictions on this construction in French provide one of the most obvious syntactic differences between French and English.

References and complications: G. Lakoff 1965.

6. Quantifier float. Optional, ungoverned.

This rule relates structures with noun phrases of the form diagrammed below, where Q= *each, all, both* and maybe some others, to structures which are identical except that the Q appears farther to the right in the structure and the preposition is absent.

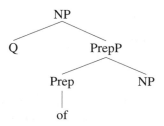

The Q cannot, however, appear to the right of a main verb, except *be*.

BOTH OF THE BOYS CAN OBVIOUSLY EAT KIMCHEE ⟷
The boys both can obviously eat kimchee.

Also: ⟷The boys can both obviously eat kimchee.
Even: ⟷ The boys can obviously both eat kimchee.
But: ←X→ *The boys can obviously eat both kimchee.

ALL OF MY RELATIVES ARE FARMERS ⟷
My relatives all are farmers.
Also: ⟷ My relatives are all farmers.

I EXPECT BOTH OF MY CLIENTS TO BE FARMERS ⟷
I expect my clients both to be farmers.
Also: ⟷ I expect my clients to both be farmers.

I WANT ALL OF MY CLIENTS TO BE FARMERS ⟷
I want my clients to be all farmers.

In the GB tradition, this phenomenon is analyzed as a movement of NP out of a Quantifier Phrase (QP).

References and complications: Postal 1974, Sag 1977, Sportiche 1988.

7. Dative movement (dative shift). Optional, governed.

A NP representing the goal or beneficiary of an action can occur as the direct object immediately following the verb, as in (a, b), or as the object of *to* or *for*, following the logical direct object, as in (c,d).

    a. Chris gave Dale a book.
    b. Chris gave a book to Dale.
    c. Dale bought Chris a book.
    d. Dale bought a book for Chris.

In relationally-based theories of grammar, dative movement is the promotion of an indirect object to direct object status, and the order of the NPs is not specified by the rule itself. Although dative movement applies to structures containing a great many verbs which mean roughly 'give', 'bring', 'send', 'tell', 'make' and 'choose', it is not governed by such verbs as *donate*, *contribute* and *mention*. It is optional except for certain kinds of idiomatic expressions, e.g., *give someone a pain*.

In transformational theories, whether *to*-dative movement and *for*-dative movement were the same phenomenon was a hotly debated issue. In most modern theories, including those in the GB-tradition (cf. Larson 1988), both dative constructions are generated independently ("base-generated"), and the verbs that governed *to*-dative movement are treated as having different entailments about their dative objects from those that governed *for*-dative movement.

Pragmatically, for both sets of verbs, the prepositionless construction implies that the speaker presupposes that the referents of the subject and indirect object arguments could have interacted at the time of the event described.

    Win this one for the Gipper. (refers to a recently deceased teammate)
    ∗Win the Gipper this one.

References and complications: Fillmore 1965, Postal 1971 (Ch. 15), Green 1974 (Ch. 3), Johnson 1978.

Inversion Constructions

8. *Be*-inversion. Optional, ungoverned.

The subject of *be* can appear after *be* while the complement of *be* appears in subject position. The complement may be a passive or progressive VP, and AP, a PP, or a predicative nominal expression (including a pseudo-cleft WH-expression—see page 163, item 27).

A COUPON GOOD FOR $1 OFF ON YOUR NEXT PURCHASE WILL
BE ENCLOSED WITH YOUR BEAUTIFUL PRINTS ⟷
Enclosed with your next purchase will be a coupon good for $1 off on
your next purchase.

SKOWRONSKI IS STEALING IT ⟷ Stealing it is Skowronski.

THE GOOD MANNERS YOU SHOWED BY WRITING TO THANK
ME ARE EQUALLY IMPORTANT ⟷
Equally important are the good manners you showed by writing to thank
me.

SAMMY SOSA IS ON DECK FOR THE CUBS ⟷
On deck for the Cubs is Sammy Sosa.

HENRY FORD'S NEPHEW WAS CHIEF EXECUTIVE OFFICER THEN
⟷ Chief executive officer then was Henry Ford's nephew.
(Cf. *Chief executive officer (then) refused to negotiate with the union.)

WHAT ATE THE EGG WAS AN OWL ⟷ An owl was what ate the egg.

WHAT CHRIS SAW WAS HIMSELF ⟷ Himself is what Chris saw.

References and complications: Stockwell, Schachter and Partee 1973; Hankamer 1974; Green 1976, 1977.

9. Subject-Auxiliary Inversion in questions. Optional, ungoverned.
    In direct questions, the subject may follow the first auxiliary verb (*be, can, have, do*, etc.) of the main clause, unless the main-clause subject is an interrogative pronoun.

SANDY CAN SWIM? ⟷ Can Sandy swim?

WHO? SANDY IS BITING __ IN THE NECK ⟷
Who is Sandy biting in the neck?

WHO? CAN SWIM ←X→ *Can who swim?[4]

WHO? SANDY WILL SAY __ LEFT ⟷ Who will Sandy say left?

If a clause has no auxiliary verb, the subject follows a "*Do*-support" *do* (see item 13 in the next section), which behaves like any other inflected auxiliary.

SANDY PLAYS THE TRUMPET ⟷
SANDY DOES PLAY THE TRUMPET ⟷
Does Sandy play the trumpet?

WHO? SANDY PICKED ⟷
WHO? SANDY DID PICK ⟷
Who did Sandy pick?

In the later GB-tradition, this phenomenon is described under the rubric of "head movement."

In some dialects, under certain conditions, embedded questions allow inversion just as direct questions do, but the intonation falls as in a statement rather than rising as in a question.

I WONDER [SANDY CAN SWIM] ⟷ I wonder can Sandy swim.

ASK THEM [WHEN THEY WILL STRIKE] ⟷ Ask them when will they strike.

In embedded yes-no questions without inversion, *if* or *whether* precedes the embedded question.

I WONDER [SANDY LEFT] ⟷ I wonder if/whether Sandy left.

[THEY LEFT] IS NOT CLEAR ⟷ Whether they left is not clear.

References: Green 1981, forthcoming.

10. Auxiliary inversion after negative adverbs. Obligatory, governed?
    The subject and the first auxiliary verb (or a supporting *do*) are inverted if a negative frequency or degree adverb precedes them (e.g., as described by Adverb Preposing–see page 160, item 23 below).

I HAVE NEVER BEEN THERE ⟷
NEVER I HAVE BEEN THERE ⟷ Never have I been there.

---

[4]This string is well-formed as an echo question: a question echoing a previous utterance by repeating it exactly, except that one phrase is replaced replaced by a WH-phrase which corresponds in all relevant properties and bears contrastive stress. (See Sadock 1969 for discussion).

RARELY SANDY STAYS AWAKE IN CLASS ⟷
Rarely does Sandy stay awake in class.

Non-negative adverbs and other kinds of negative adverbs do not support inversion:

SOMETIMES I EAT WHEATIES ←X→
*Sometimes do I eat Wheaties.

UNFORTUNATELY HE IS TOO LATE ←X→
*Unfortunately is he too late.

In archaic English, this inversion is licensed by positive frequency and degree adverbs, and in even more archaic language, by manner adverbs:

OFTEN I VISITED THE INHABITANTS OF THAT GLOOMY VIL-
LAGE ⟷
Often did I visit the inhabitants of that gloomy village.

PARTICULARLY HE LIKED ITS DESCRIPTIONS OF RECENT AC-
QUISITIONS ⟷
Particularly did he like its descriptions of recent acquisitions.

UNHAPPILY HE WALKED HOME ⟷ ?Unhappily did he walk home.

It is not clear whether inversion after such negative expressions as *nor, neither; hardly...when; no sooner...than*; negative NPs like *not a word, under no circumstances*, and *only NP* are part of the same phenomenon. All of these constructions and Subject-auxiliary inversion treat pronoun subjects the same as any other subject.

References and complications: Green 1977, 1982a, 1985.

11. Main verb inversion after locative and directional adverbs and phrases. Optional, governed?

When a directional adverb or adverbial phrase (*Up, Out; Into NP*) or a locative adverb or adverbial phrase (*Here, There; In NP*) is in clause-initial position, the subject and the verb, with all auxiliaries, may be inverted. There is no *do*-support.

THE CAVALRY RODE INTO THE VALLEY ⟷
INTO THE VALLEY THE CAVALRY RODE ⟷
Into the valley rode the cavalry.

[...] UPON WHICH A BALD EAGLE RESTING ON A NEST OF CRISCROSSED BATS WAS DEPICTED. ⟷
[...], upon which was depicted a bald eagle resting on a nest of criscrossed bats.

It is not clear whether all of these cases are properly considered the same phenomenon, as they have differing constraints and governing classes. For instance, inversion is obligatory if the main verb is *be*:

*In the garden a white rabbit was.
In the garden was a white rabbit.

This construction is distinguished from inversion after negative expressions in that the "pivot" is not just the first auxiliary verb, but the main verb and all of its auxiliaries, and it does not license inversion of pronominal subjects.

INTO THE VALLEY THEY RODE ←X→ *Into the valley rode they.

Because this construction allows logical subjects and verb phrase modifiers to appear in non-canonical positions, it finds use in a variety of "niche" registers, both oral and written, to exploit the prominent clause-initial and clause-final positions.

References and complications: Green 1977, 1982a, 1985a, 1985b Birner 1992, 1994; Birner and Ward 1998.

12. Inversion with direct quotations. Optional, ungoverned?
     The subject of a verb of saying may follow the verb if the direct object quotation precedes the subject, as long as the subject is not a pronoun. There is no *do*-support.

"FARQUHAR'S A FLUMMER!" THE OLD MAN SHOUTED ⟷
"Farquhar's a flummer!" shouted the old man.

"YOUR HAIR'S ON FIRE!" HE SHOUTED ←X→
*"Your hair's on fire!" shouted he.

In contemporary standard written English, subject and quotation verb are inverted only if the direct quotation precedes the subject and verb of saying, but in older stages, this may not have been necessary.

Quoth the raven, "Nevermore."

In archaic and some casual speech, pronoun subjects invert, both before and after the quotation.

Says he: "I'm gonna beat you to a pulp."
"You and which army?" says I.

References and complications: Banfield 1973; Hermon 1979; Green 1980, 1982a, 1985.

Insertion Rules

13. *Do*-support.
   In a number of circumstances where the subject is licensed to follow an auxiliary verb, structures which wouldn't otherwise have an auxiliary verb have the appropriate form of *do* as an auxiliary verb. Whether this was the effect of a *do*-support rule inserting *do*, or of an underlying *do* which would be deleted except when it preceded a non-auxiliary was a matter of some debate among standard-theory syntacticians. Some examples of "*do*-support":

Did Sara swim the English Channel?
Only once did he try to trick us.
Thus did the hen reward Beecher.
Sandy knew the answer, and so did Chris.
Sandy knew the answer, and Chris did too.
Margaret knew the answer, as did Sara.

References and complications: Green and Morgan 1976, Akmajian and Heny 1975, Ross 1972a, Akmajian and Wasow 1975.

14. Existential *there*-insertion. Optional, governed.
   An indefinite subject of *be* (e.g., *a boy, three outhouses*, but not *the boy* or *those three outhouses*) can follow *be*, if the expletive *there* is in the canonical subject position.

A SALESMAN IS AT THE DOOR ⟷ There is a salesman at the door.
SIX PEOPLE WERE NAMED TO A COMMISSION TO STUDY THE PROBLEM ⟷
There were six people named to a commission to study the problem.

It is immaterial whether the *be* is a main verb or an auxiliary verb.

References and complications: Borkin 1971, Milsark 1974, Napoli and Rando 1978.

15. Presentational *there*-insertion. Optional, governed.

This phenomenon is similar to existential *there*-insertion except that it is licensed by a wider class of verbs, and involves both definite and indefinite NPs. In addition, the canonical subject NP follows the entire VP, not just the verb.

> A LARGE PACKAGE MARKED "PERISHABLE" WILL ARRIVE BY FEDEX. ⟷
> There will arrive by FedEx a large package marked "PERISHABLE."

> THE LINGUIST WE HAD BEEN SPEAKING OF SAT IN THE COR-NER ⟷
> There sat in the corner the linguist we had been speaking of.

Unlike existential *there*-insertion, this phenomenon is limited to cases where a locative or directional complement is part of the VP.

> THE LINGUIST WE WERE SPEAKING OF REALIZED ITS SIGNIF-ICANCE IMMEDIATELY ←X→
> *There realized its significance immediately the linguist we were speaking of.

> TWO OR THREE NERVOUS PARENTS PACED IN THE ANTEROOM ⟷ There paced in the anteroom two or three nervous parents.

> TWO OR THREE NERVOUS PARENTS PACED THE FLOOR ←X→
> *There paced the floor two or three nervous parents.

The more obviously locative or directional the verb is, the better the construction sounds:

> There lay/?slept/??dreamed in the corner a raggedy young man.

References and complications: Aissen 1975, Hankamer 1977.

Copying Rules

16. Verb agreement. Obligatory, ungoverned.

Inflections on a finite verb reflect the number and person (and in some languages, gender) of its nominative or absolutive argument (and in some languages, its object and other adjuncts):

I BE WRITING $\longleftrightarrow$ I am writing.
HE BE WRITING $\longleftrightarrow$ He is writing.
THEY BE WRITING $\longleftrightarrow$ They are writing.

In some languages (e.g., Portuguese), inflection on non-finite forms may do the same thing.

How the number of the subject is computed is far from being a simple matter. Questions and doubts arise particularly in cases like:

To the states BELONG the power to regulate education of the young.
Either three men or a woman BE in the room.
There BE a man and three children in the room.

From the earliest days of generative grammar, the analysis of verb agreement has involved features. Standard-theory syntacticians debated whether verb agreement was a cyclic rule.

References and complications: Morgan 1972b, 1972c, 1984, 1985; Pullum 1984; Pollard and Sag 1994; Chomsky 1995, Morgan and Green (forthcoming).

17. Tag question. Optional? governed?
    This is one of the earliest phenomena studied in the history of modern transformational grammar; it was used to argue for underlying *you* and *will* in imperative sentences. The traditional description of this phenomenon says that corresponding to every declarative or imperative sentence, there is a sentence which is identical except that adjoined at the right is a copy of the first auxiliary verb (or *do* with appropriate tense and number), and a pronoun appropriate to refer to the subject. The tag auxiliary is negative if the verb is not negated, and positive if the verb is negated.

JOAN IS SMART $\longleftrightarrow$ Joan is smart, isn't she?

YOU CAN ANNOUNCE THAT SANDY ISN'T HERE $\longleftrightarrow$
You can announce that Sandy isn't here, can't you?

SANDY AND CHRIS HAVEN'T ARRIVED YET $\longleftrightarrow$
Sandy and Chris haven't arrived yet, have they?

I CHEERED YOU UP $\longleftrightarrow$ I cheered you up, didn't I?

COME IN ⟷ Come in, won't you.

This characterization fails to describe such sentences as:

I guess it'll be OK, won't it?
Shut up, will you.
Turn the record over, could you.
Sandy's a narc, is he?
∗Here comes the bus, doesn't it?
I don't suppose the Yankees will win, will they?

This construction seems to be specific to English, although many languages have idiomatic constructions (or particles) which serve the same discourse purposes. With different prosodies, tag questions may be used to ask confirmatory questions (where the addressee is expected to verify the proposition put forth by the asker), as well as to pressure the addressee into conceding or admitting that an ostensibly asserted proposition is true.

References and complications: Bolinger 1967; Postal 1969; R. Lakoff 1969, 1972a, 1972b, 1973; Borkin 1971; Green 1975.

18. Right dislocation. Optional, ungoverned.
     An NP may appear in clause-final position, instead of in its normal position, where the corresponding definite pronoun appears.

THE COPS SPOKE TO THE JANITOR ABOUT THE ROBBERY YESTERDAY
     ⟷ They spoke to the janitor about the robbery yesterday, the cops.
Or: ⟷ The cops spoke to the janitor about it yesterday, the robbery.

THAT THE COPS WILL SPEAK TO THE JANITOR ABOUT THE ROBBERY TOMORROW GOES WITHOUT SAYING
     ⟷ That they will speak to the janitor about the robbery tomorrow,the cops, goes without saying.
But: ←X→ ∗That they will speak to the janitor about the robbery tomorrow goes without saying, the cops.

References and complications: Ross 1967/83.

Deletion Rules

19. Agent-deletion. Optional, ungoverned?

The logical subject of a passive sentence may be left unspecified. In modern theories, there will simply be no agent argument, but in classical transformational grammar, there was a rule to delete the passive *by* as well as its agent NP object in a passive sentence, if the NP was an indefinite pronoun (*someone* or *something*).

> CHRIS WAS RUN OVER BY SOMEONE/SOMETHING ⟶
> Chris was run over.

This rule would have been considered to be governed only to the extent that there are a few verbs (e.g., *rumor*) whose passive form does not allow an agent phrase. Use of this construction is motivated by a desire not to name the agent (whether out of ignorance of the agent's identity, desire not to represent the agent as responsible, or desire to make the act seem less personal). In many languages, the agent of a passive verb is never expressed.

References and complications: Leskosky 1973, Gazdar 1982.

20. Truncation. Optional, governed.

In casual discourse, certain sentence-initial subject pronouns and/or auxiliaries, and sometimes even determiners, may be absent under some rather complicated conditions. There is no identity requirement on their absence.

ARE YOU GOING TO THE PARTY	⟷	You going to the party?
Or:	⟷	Going to the party?
WILL YOU BE GOING TO THE PARTY	⟷	You be going to the party?
But:	←X→	*Be going to the party?
And:	←X→	*Will you going to the party?
I HAVE GOT TO GO NOW	⟷	Got to go now.
But:	←X→	*Have got to go now.
MY/THE CAR'S IN THE SHOP	⟷	Car's in the shop.

References and complications: Schmerling 1973, Cote 1996.

21. Object deletion. Optional, governed.

Some transitive verbs occur without objects in contexts where it will be understood that the referent of an implied object is one that is predictable for the meaning of that verb in that context. Thus:

I'VE ALREADY EATEN [A MEAL] ⟷ I've already eaten.

THEY DON'T DRINK [ALCOHOLIC BEVERAGES] ⟷
They don't drink.

CHRIS READ [BOOKS] FOR 3 HOURS LAST NIGHT ⟷
Chris read for 3 hours last night.

HAVE YOU EVER RAISED [CROPS] ←X→ *Have you ever raised?

GHOSTS FRIGHTEN [PEOPLE] ←X→ *Ghosts frighten.

It is now considered doubtful that this is a syntactic phenomenon, but in the
early days of transformational grammar it was taken to be. More likely, the
interpretation of an object is pragmatic, like the interpretation of unspecified
subjects of non-finite complement verb phrases in sentences like:

Kim suggested __ putting pickles in the ice cream.
__ Amusing Dana's father will be difficult.
It would be unwise __ to tickle Dana's father.
Kim chose a book __ to read to their children.

The phenomenon is lexical in that it is not found with all transitive verbs.

References and complications: Lees 1960, Chomsky 1965, Newmeyer 1969,
Gazdar 1981, Bach 1982, Cote 1996, Williams 1995.

Coreference Rules

22. Clause-mate reflexivization. Ungoverned, obligatory.
    If two coreferential NPs are in the same simple clause (more formally: if
they command each other), the one that follows will have the reflexive form
that corresponds in person, number, and gender to the one that precedes.

Chris likes himself/*themselves.
John$_i$ talked to Mary$_j$ about himself$_i$/herself$_j$.
*John$_i$ thinks that Mary$_j$ likes himself$_i$.

In the earliest days of generative grammar, reflexive pronouns were licensed by a feature-changing transformational rule. Since the 1970s, they
have been taken to be generated like any other lexical item. Chomsky (1981)

made their analysis a central point of his Binding Theory.

References and complications: Lees and Klima 1963, Morgan 1970, Postal 1971, Kuno 1972, Jackendoff 1972, Harris 1976, Chomsky 1981.

More definitions

BOUNDED. Ross (1967) argued that transformational rules that reordered an element rightward (like Heavy-NP-Shift and Right Dislocation) were all **upper-bounded**, in that the elements could not be displaced farther than the end of their own clause, but that some leftward "movements", like WH-rel positioning and Adverb Preposing, might or might not be upper-bounded, and could in principle relate an item low in the structure directly to a preceding "landing site" many clauses higher. Since the sequence of constituents between the underlying and surface positions of the moved item could be arbitrarily long, dependencies between the underlying and surface positions were called "unbounded". The formulation of a rule describing an unbounded dependency requires the use of essential variables (see page 118), and the rule was said to apply over a variable. Since then, linguists (e.g., Chomsky 1977) have taken the position that all transformational rules are **bounded** in that they may only relate elements to positions within their clause or in the next higher clause. This resulted in postulating that unbounded dependencies arise through successive bounded movements from complementizer position to complementizer position. As seen in Chapter 7, non-transformational theories likewise describe unbounded dependencies in terms of a series of linked local dependencies.

CHOMSKY-ADJUNCTION. When a node A is Chomsky-adjoined to a node B, A is the sole sister of B and the node that dominates both A and B has the same syntactic category as B. For example, Chomsky-adjoining a node A to S on the left in a structure like (a) defines a structure like (b):

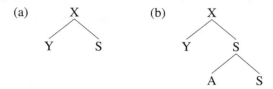

PIED PIPING CONVENTION. In many languages, if a NP or PP, X_2, contains a relative or interrogative word x_1, it counts as relative or interrogative itself, provided that every node intervening between x_1 and X_2 is itself a NP or PP. In the context of the movement metaphor that was current then, it was natural for

Ross (1967) to call this apparent attraction of higher structure **Pied Piping**. Some examples:

REPORTS$_i$ [THE GOVERNMENT PRESCRIBES THE HEIGHT OF THE LETTERING ON THE COVERS OF WHICH$_i$] ARE INVARIABLY BORING

⟷ Reports which the government prescribes the height of the lettering on the covers of are invariably boring. (No Pied Piping)

OR: ⟷ Reports the covers of which the government prescribes the height of the lettering on are invariably boring. (Pied Piping of 1 NP)

OR: ⟷ Reports the height of the lettering on the covers of which the government prescribes are invariably boring. (Pied Piping of 3 NPs)

Pied Piping may be *de facto* obligatory through the interaction of relative clause principles with other principles. For example, in a language like French that does not allow prepositions to appear without objects, the Pied Piped form is the only grammatical one. Even in English, which generally allows prepositions to be "stranded," Pied Piping is required under some conditions, as demonstrated by the following examples.

The time at which you depart is 11:00.
∗The time which you depart at is 11:00.
The manner in which he spoke shocked many people.
∗The manner which he spoke in shocked many people.

Multiple-Clause Phenomena

Coreference Rules

1. Pronominalization. Obligatory, ungoverned.

A noun phrase NP$_a$ can serve as an antecedent for (i.e., license its being taken to refer to the same individual, object, or notion as) a definite pronoun with the same person, number, and gender in the same sentence if NP$_a$ precedes NP$_p$. An antecedent NP, NP$_a$, may follow a coreferential pronoun NP$_p$ only if NP$_p$ does not command NP$_a$.

Some examples:

Sam$_i$ brushed his teeth after he$_i$ got up.
(*Sam* precedes *he*.)
∗He$_i$ brushed his teeth after Sam$_i$ got up.
(*He* precedes and commands *Sam*.)

After Sam$_i$ got up, he$_i$ brushed his teeth.
(*Sam* precedes *he*.

After he$_i$ got up, Sam$_i$ brushed his teeth.
(*He* precedes but doesn't command *Sam*.)
Sam$_i$ thinks he$_i$ is late.
(*Sam* precedes *he*.)
*He$_i$ thinks that Sam$_i$ is late.
(*He* precedes and commands *Sam*.)
The claim that Sam$_i$ is ugly worries him$_i$.
(*Sam* precedes *him*.)
The claim that he$_i$ is ugly worries Sam$_i$.
(*He* precedes but doesn't command *Sam*.)

The pronoun and antecedent may be arbitrarily far apart as long as the precedence and command conditions are satisfied.

Sam$_i$ thinks it is possible that Dale told me that you thought it would be easy to reach him$_i$.

In some languages, this relationship is expressed by the absence of a noun phrase where English would have a pronoun. These languages are sometimes referred to as "pro-drop languages" with "zero" or "null" pronouns.

Some early treatments (e.g., Langacker 1966, Ross 1969) had pronominalization as a transformation, with full NPs underlying pronouns. Ross (1969b) argued that pronominalization is cyclic (see Chapter 5), to account for the unexpected unacceptability of examples like:

*Realizing that Oscar$_i$ had bad breath didn't bother him$_i$.

The unexpected acceptability of another sentence prompted arguments (Lakoff 1976, Postal 1970) that it must be post-cyclic.

Who from Flora$_i$'s hometown did Sam think she$_i$ would marry?

The resolution was a paradigm-bending consensus that "pronominalization" was not a transformational "operation" at all, but a constraint on structural representations. In the GB tradition, pronominalization facts are the domain of Binding Principle B.

The indefinite pronoun *one* requires a preceding indefinite NP$_a$ as antecedent. The pronoun *one* has the same sense (but not reference) as the nominal head of NP$_a$.

When Sandy found a music box that played *Feelings*, Chris looked on eBay for one.

Indefinite pronouns are more restricted in their syntactic relation to their antecedent than definite pronouns.

??When one became available, Lou bought a Corgi.
A nurse said that one [nurse] would take us to the recovery room.

References and complications: Langacker 1966, Ross 1969b; G. Lakoff 1968, 1976; Postal 1970, McCawley 1968a, Karttunen 1971, Jackendoff 1972, Kuno 1972, 1975; Kantor 1977, Chomsky 1981, Pollard and Sag 1994.

2. Sentence pronominalization (S-deletion). Optional, ungoverned.
    If a proposition is expressed as a clause or non-finite VP, a second reference to it may have the form of the referential pronoun *it*.

LOU SAID THAT MAX LEFT, BUT I DON'T BELIEVE THAT MAX LEFT ⟷ Lou said that Max left, but I don't believe it. [that Max left]

Chris won't win the race, since the fortune-tellers have predicted it. [that Chris will win...]
Jo wants to climb the pole, but Lou thinks it will scare their mom. [Jo climbing the pole]

The *it* may refer to the positive form of a proposition even if the sentential antecedent is superficially negative.

Chris won't win the race, even if the fortune-tellers have predicted it. [that Chris will win...]

The pronoun may precede or follow its antecedent.

Although Chris didn't believe it, I told him that the library was closed.
Chris didn't realize it, but he had created a whole new field.

References and complications: G. Lakoff 1966, 1969; Hankamer and Sag 1976.

3. Equi-NP-Deletion (control, "big" PRO).
    A subject NP in a non-finite complement clause may be unexpressed, and interpreted as coreferential with a NP in the embedding clause. When the complement clause follows the coreferential NP in the main clause, Equi is governed by verbs of commitment, influence, or emotional orientation that take propositional arguments (e.g., *promise, try; order, persuade; want, hate*).

I TRIED [I GO]$_S$ $\longleftrightarrow$ I tried to go.

[CHRIS$_i$'S BEING FIRED]$_S$ ANNOYED CHRIS$_i$ $\longleftrightarrow$
Being fired annoyed Chris.

SANDY PERSUADED CHRIS$_i$ [CHRIS$_i$ GO] $\longleftrightarrow$
Sandy persuaded Chris to go.

CHRIS$_i$ PROMISED [CHRIS$_i$ GO] $\longleftrightarrow$ Chris promised to go.

I WANT [I GO]$_S$ $\longleftrightarrow$ I want to go.

I INSIST [I GO]$_S$ $\leftarrow$X$\rightarrow$ *I insist to go.

The analysis of this construction is the focus of the GB Control Theory.. The facts that must be accounted for are considerably more complicated than they seemed in the early days of generative grammar. When the complement clause precedes the controller NP in the main clause, Equi appears to be ungoverned and there may be no syntactic constraint on the interpretation of the unexpressed subject.

Letting the cat walk on the table always bothered Chris. [Subject of *let* could be anyone.]
Letting the cat walk on the table implied there were other options. [Subject of *let* could be anyone.]

When the controller precedes, the coreferential NP is unexpressed (unless the verb also allows Raising, e.g., with *want* and *expect*. When the controller follows, the coreferential NP may be expressed.

References and complications: Rosenbaum 1967; Morgan 1970, Postal 1970, 1974; Borkin 1972, Green 1973b, Fodor 1974, Manzini 1983, Sag and Pollard 1991, Pollard and Sag 1994, Williams 1995.

4. Super-equi. Optional, apparently ungoverned.
    An unexpressed subject NP of a non-finite complement is understood as coreferential to a NP in an arbitrarily higher S, i.e., over a variable. In other words, the antecedent NP need not be in the immediately higher clause, but may be separated from the non-finite verb by any number of intervening clauses.

CHRIS$_i$ BELIEVED [IT WAS POSSIBLE [IT WOULD BE NECESSARY [FOR CHRIS$_i$ TO TIE HIS OWN SHOE LACES]]]
⟶ Chris believed it was possible that it would be necessary to tie his own shoe laces.

References and complications: Grinder 1970, 1971; Kimball 1971, Neubauer 1972, Green 1973b, Clements 1974, Hayes 1976b, Kuno 1974.

5. Purpose infinitive
   Purpose infinitives always exhibit a gap which is interpreted as coreferential with an argument NP:

Kim bought *War and Peace*$_i$ to read __$_i$ to the kids.
Kim bought a book$_i$ for Sandy to read __$_i$ to the kids.
Kim hired a student$_i$ __$_i$ to file the offprints.
That book$_i$ is available to read __$_i$ to the kids.

Purpose infinitives have different properties depending on whether they modify predicates or referential expressions. Purpose infinitives that affect the interpretation of VPs are governed by predicates that entail possession:

I bought it to read to the children.
*I saw it to read to the children.
The oxygen is there to revive astonished clients with.
*The oxygen is odorless to revive astonished clients with.

If there is a subject gap in addition to a non-subject gap, the subject gap is pragmatically controlled; that is, it may be coreferential to a preceding NP, or may have a discourse antecedent:

Chris$_i$ bought a book$_j$ __ to distract him$_i$ with __$_j$.
[i.e., for someone indicated in the context to distract him with]

Similar infinitives which modify nominal expressions are similar to adverbial purpose infinitives in having a gap coreferential to a preceding NP, but with oblique gaps they allow an overt relative pronoun:

Kim saw a fountain in which to cool her toes __.
A book with which to distract the kids __ would make a nice gift.
*Kim knows a man (for) who to amuse Sandy.
*Kim saw a book which to read __ to Sandy.
Kim saw a fountain (for Sandy) to cool her toes in __.
Kim lost the book to read __ to the children.

References and complications: Baxter 1999.

Clause-Membership Alternations

6. Subject raising. Optional, governed

a. Into subject position (SSR, A-Raising)

The subject of a clausal subject argument of a verb which does not have a sentential direct object appears as the subject argument of the verb, as shown schematically below. The clausal argument whose subject is raised appears as an infinitive VP at the end of the clause. The first transformational analysis of this construction (Rosenbaum 1967) invoked extraposition[5] of the clausal subject before Raising; Rosenbaum referred to Raising as *it*-Replacement.

[CHRIS WIN] IS LIKELY ⟷ Chris is likely to win.

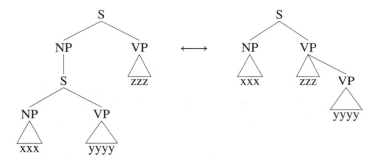

Raising into subject position is governed, and optional for *be likely*, *be certain*, *seem*, *happen*, and the like. It is obligatory for *tend* and *begin*, but not possible for *be possible*, *be obvious*, and others. Within the GB tradition, it is considered to be an instance of A-movement.

Pragmatically, there is a presupposition that the referent of the subject argument did or would interact with the referent of the experiencer NP in the world defined by the event described in the infinitive verb phrase.

It seems to me that Napoleon loved peace.
!Napoleon seems to me to have loved peace.

It struck me that Julius Caesar was anti-democratic.
!Julius Caesar struck me as anti-democratic.

b. Into object position. (SOR, B-raising)

The subject of a propositional object complement of a transitive verb appears as the direct object of that verb.

---

[5] See item 15 below.

CHRIS WANTS [I GO] ⟷ Chris wants me to go.
CHRIS$_i$ BELIEVES [CHRIS$_i$ BE SHY] ⟷ Chris believes himself to be shy.

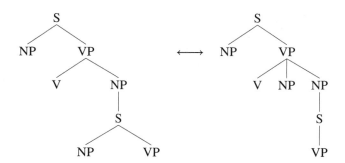

Raising to object is governed by verbs of wanting, thinking, and many others. It is optional for most, but obligatory for some, e.g., *consider*. The GB analysis of this structure (dating back to Chomsky 1973) is that the postverbal NP is not an object, but a subject exceptionally marked for accusative case.

Pragmatically, there is a presupposition that the referent of the accusative NP did or would interact with the referent of the subject NP in the world defined by the event described.

> Patton found that Napoleon was a vicious man.
> !Patton found Napoleon to have been a vicious man.

> I will ask that Chris leave.
> (=X=) I will ask Chris to leave.

References and complications: Rosenbaum 1967; McCawley 1970, Andrews 1971, Chomsky 1973, 1981; Postal 1974, Borkin 1974, Sheintuch 1976, Steever 1977, Schmerling 1978, Marantz 1991.

7. *Tough*-movement. Optional, governed.

A non-subject argument in the propositional subject complement of certain predicates appears as the subject of that predicate, and the remainder of the clausal complement is a sister of the governing phrase. This is represented schematically below.

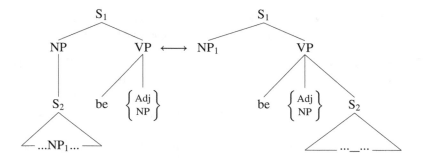

In Rosenbaum's (1967) analysis, extraposition of the subject complement was separate from the raising of a non-subject from it.

The governing term is an evaluative adjective or noun such as *impossible, easy, hard, nice; chore, fun, cinch, drag, a joy*. Non-evaluative predicates like *possible, task* do not license *tough*-movement.

[FOR ME TO LOOK AFTER SAM] IS A JOY ⟷
Sam is a joy for me to look after.

[TO SEE [THAT JOE LIKES YOU]] IS EASY ⟷
That Joe likes you is easy to see.

[FOR ME TO TALK TO CHRIS] IS IMPOSSIBLE ⟷
Chris is impossible for me to talk to.

The target NP can be embedded deep within the complement proposition as long as all of the intervening verbs are non-finite.

Chris is easy to arrange to talk to __.
Lou is hard to persuade anyone to try to arrange to talk to __.
*Chris is easy to see that Lou admires __.

Pragmatically, this construction differs from truth-conditional paraphrases in that it implies that the property denoted by the *tough*-class predicate is an inherent property of the derived subject of that predicate.

It is hard to play sonatas on this violin.
Sonatas are hard to play on this violin.
This violin is hard to play sonatas on.

The dirt on my glasses makes it impossible to read my notes.
The dirt on my glasses makes my notes impossible to read.

References and complications: Rosenbaum 1967, Ross 1967/83, Morgan 1968, Partee 1971, Postal 1971, Berman 1973, Nanni 1980.

8. Negative transportation (Negative raising, *not*-Hopping). Optional, governed.

A negative operator which is logically construed with an embedded clause may belong syntactically to an embedding VP headed by a predicate in the governing class.

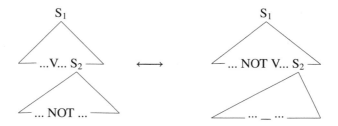

CHRIS THINKS LOU DOES NOT HAVE AN IOTA OF COMMON SENSE ⟷
Chris doesn't think Lou has an iota of common sense.

Compare:

∗Lou has an iota of common sense.
∗Chris doesn't realize Lou has an iota of common sense.

The governing predicate in S_1 must be a non-factive predicate of mental state: *think, want, expect, intend, likely, seem*, and many others, but not *know, hear, say* or *probable*.

References and complications: R. Lakoff 1969; Horn 1971, 1975, 1979, 1989; Green 1974, Halpern 1976.

Question Rules

9. Constituent questions (WH-Movement). Obligatory in embedded structures, ungoverned.

An interrogative pronoun may appear Chomsky-adjoined at the beginning of the interrogative clause where it is syntactically licensed:

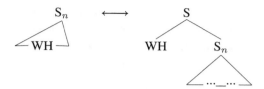

An interrogative clause is (a) the main clause in a direct question, or (b) a subordinate clause which is the subject or object (direct or oblique) of a verb implying a question, however indirectly.

DANA HIT WHO? IN THE NOSE ⟷ Who? Dana hit in the nose

JO ASKED DANA HIT WHO? IN THE NOSE ⟷
Jo asked who Dana hit in the nose.

JO CLAIMED DANA HIT WHO? IN THE NOSE ←X→
*Jo claimed who Dana hit in the nose.

I AM CURIOUS ABOUT [DANA HIT WHO?] ⟷ I am curious about who Dana hit.

[DANA HIT WHO?] IS OBVIOUS ⟷ Who Dana hit is obvious.

As with WH-relative constructions (see 12 below), it may be that this construction is best described in terms of a class of (interrogative) pronouns in structures where a complementizer like *that* or *if* is licensed to appear. This construction defines an unbounded dependency, and is subject to Pied Piping.

I KNOW [JAN TOLD SANDY [KIM SAID [YOU TRIED TO DO WHAT? LAST SUMMER IN A GOLF CART]]] ⟷
I know what Jan told Sandy Kim said you tried to do last summer.

I WILL ASK [THESE BOOKS WERE WRITTEN BY WHO?]
⟷ I will ask who these books were written by __ .
or ⟷ I will ask by whom these books were written __ . (Pied Piping)

References and complications: Baker 1968, 1970a, Bach 1971, Langacker 1974, Bresnan 1972, Kuno and Robinson 1972, Chomsky 1986b.

10. Sluicing. Optional, ungoverned.

An indirect question complement may consist of just a question word as long as the context allows a complete question clause to be reconstructed. The indirect question must correspond to a clause occurring in previous discourse, except that the node corresponding to the interrogative pronoun will be an indefinite NP.

THE PAPER SAID THE MAN WAS SELLING SOMETHING, AL-THOUGH IT WAS UNCLEAR [HE WAS SELLING WHAT?] ⟷ The paper said the man was selling something, although it was unclear what.

SOMEBODY SAW SANDY, BUT I DON'T KNOW [WHO? SAW SANDY] ⟷ Somebody saw Sandy, but I don't know who.

SANDY WANTED SOMEONE TO LEAVE; GUESS [HE WANTED [WHO? TO LEAVE]] ⟷ Sandy wanted someone to leave; guess who.

The corresponding indefinite clause need not be in the same sentence, nor even attributable to the same speaker:

A: Sandy wanted someone to leave.
B: Will you tell me who? (= 'will you tell me who Sandy wanted to leave?')

Sluicing is thus a discourse-licensed construction (the domain of its structural description is a stretch of discourse), not a sentence-level rule. See the discussion below on discourse deletions. Sluicing is generally appropriate only if it is assumed that someone relevant to the discourse wants to know the answer to the indirect question. Thus:

!Somebody took my book, and I can tell who.
Somebody took your book, and only I know who.

This rule has counterparts in several European languages.

References and complications: Ross 1969a; Green 1981, forthcoming.

Relative Clause Constructions

The relative clause structure referred to in these rules is a NP containing a head N' and a sister S (the relative clause), which contains a NP coreferential to the dominating NP. In the diagram below, the circled N' is the head.

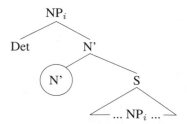

It continues to be a matter of debate whether relative clauses are adjuncts to N' or NP.

11. Relative gaps (NP deletion). Ungoverned.
A restrictive relative clause structure may appear without any relative pronoun, and have just a gap where a NP coreferential to the dominating NP would be expected.

I CAUGHT THE KITTEN$_i$ [(THAT) CYNDY BROUGHT HOME
WHICH$_i$] $\longleftrightarrow$ I caught the kitten (that) Cyndy brought home.

This construction is found in many languages. Often such relative clauses are introduced with the general subordinate clause complementizer (*that* in English). It continues to be debated whether the *that* in such constructions in English is a complementizer, or in fact, a relative pronoun. If it is not a pronoun, there must be a principle that entails the absence of a complementizer when a relative pronoun is present.

THE MAN$_i$ [THAT CHRIS HIT WHO$_i$] IS SICK
$\longleftrightarrow$ THE MAN WHO [THAT CHRIS HIT] IS SICK
$\longleftrightarrow$ The man who Chris hit is sick.

An alternative analysis of this construction is that the relative pronoun appears in the place of the complementizer:

THE MAN$_i$ [THAT CHRIS HIT WHO$_i$] IS SICK $\longleftrightarrow$
The man who Chris hit is sick.

Either analysis will explain why Pied Piping of NPs is only found with WH-relatives:

I FOUND THE RESTAURANT$_i$ [THAT THEY ATE AT WHICH$_i$]
←X→ *I found the restaurant at that they ate __.

According to both, *that* is a complementizer, not a relative pronoun, hence not subject to displacement, let alone Pied Piping.

The deletion analysis must rule out sentences with both WH-word and *that* by stipulating that the rule is obligatory if a relative pronoun is present. The replacement analysis guarantees that the sequence won't occur by requiring the WH-phrase to occur in place of the *that*.

The presence of *that* is generally optional in relative clauses with no WH-phrase.

I found the restaurant (that) they ate at.

"Bare" relative clauses are generally considered unacceptable if the missing coreferential NP is the subject of the highest S in the relative clause. Thus they are acceptable if the missing coreferential NP is an object.

The man [Chris called __] is here.

And they are fine if the missing coreferential NP is the subject of a lower S:

The man Harry thinks [__ saw Chris] just arrived.

The problematic case is when the missing coreferential NP is the subject of the highest S in the relative clause:

*The man [__ saw Chris] is here.
The man who saw Chris is here.
The man that [__ saw Chris] is here.

In some dialects, however, some semantically indefinite NPs may head bare relative clause missing their highest subjects:

Anyone wants to play football will have to maintain at least a C average.
The man runs for president had better be rich.

Deletion of the relative clause complementizer is found in many languages, including Chinese.

References and complications: Morgan 1972a; Perlmutter 1972; McCawley 1978b, 1981; Gazdar 1981; Sag 1997.

12. WH-headed relative clauses (WH movement). Obligatory, ungoverned.
 A relative pronoun may appear as a Chomsky-adjoined left sister of a relative clause with a gap. Such relative clauses may be either restrictive or non-restrictive.

[THE MAN$_i$ [CHRIS PHONED WHO$_i$] IS SICK] $\longleftrightarrow$
The man who Chris phoned is sick.

[SMITH$_i$ [DALE WAS VISITING WHO$_i$] JUST WON THE LOTTERY]
$\longleftrightarrow$ Smith, who Dale was visiting, just won the lottery.

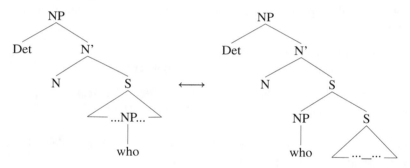

This is an unbounded dependency construction; the relative pronoun may be any number of clauses "down" from the head NP.

THE MAN$_i$ [DALE THINKS [LOU SAID [THE FBI BELIEVES CHRIS WANTED [TO KIDNAP WHO$_i$]]]] ORDERED CHOP SUEY $\longleftrightarrow$
The man who Dale thinks Lou said the FBI believes Chris wanted to kidnap ordered chop suey.

This construction is common to many languages.

References and complications: Ross 1967/83, Sec. 4.3; Morgan 1972a and other papers in *The Chicago Which Hunt*; Bresnan 1972; McCawley 1978b, 1981; Kayne 1994, Sag 1997.

13. Relative infinitives. Ungoverned.

Relative infinitives are similar to purpose infinitives in having a gap coreferential to a preceding NP, but with oblique gaps, they may have an overt relative pronoun:

> Kim saw a fountain in which to cool her toes _.
> A book with which to distract the kids _ would make a nice gift.
> *Kim knows a man (for) who to amuse Sandy.
> *Kim saw a book which to read _ to Sandy.
> Kim saw a fountain (for Sandy) to cool her toes in _.
> Kim lost the book to read _ to the children.

Pied Piping is obligatory.

> *Kim saw a fountain which to cool her toes in _.

Relative infinitives differ from purpose infinitives in that, like restrictive relative clauses, they are understood as modifying nominal expressions, and do not occur with proper noun or definite pronoun heads. They do not allow overt subjects.

> *I saw it to read _ to the children.
> *I saw a fountain in which for Sandy to cool her toes _.

References and complications: Green 1973a, 1992; Berman 1974c; Bach 1982; Ladusaw and Dowty 1985; Sag 1997; Baxter 1999.

14. Reduced relative clause (WH + *be* deletion; also WH-is deletion, or Whiz-deletion). Optional, ungoverned.

A relative clause may consist of just a predicate complement of *be*, regardless of type.

> THEY WANT TO HIRE SOMEONE WHO IS SMALL ⟷
> They want to hire someone small.

> A VASE WHICH WAS FROM INDIA WAS BROKEN ⟷
> A vase from India was broken.

> BESSIE, WHO IS OUR RED COW, DIED ⟷
> Bessie, our red cow, died.

> CHRIS SMITH, WHO IS 31 AND BALDING, TURNED THE CORNER INTO WORDSWORTH LANE ⟷
> Chris Smith, 31 and balding, turned the corner into Wordsworth Lane.

THE MAN WHO IS EATING THE POTATOES ROBBED THE BANK
$\longleftrightarrow$ The man eating the potatoes robbed the bank.

THE MAN WHO WAS THOUGHT TO HAVE ROBBED THE BANK
HAS DISAPPEARED $\longleftrightarrow$
The man thought to have robbed the bank has disappeared.

In English, nominal complements licensed in this construction have the intonation and interpretation of non-restrictive relative clause. Otherwise, the intonation and interpretation are restrictive.

*The woman a trial lawyer is carrying a canvas briefcase
The woman, a trial lawyer, is carrying a canvas briefcase.

References and complications: Borkin 1971, Sag 1997.

Clause Position Alternations

15. Extraposition. Normally optional, possibly obligatory for a few verbs; to that extent, governed.

A verb that subcategorizes for a clausal subject with the form of a *that*-clause or an infinitive may appear with a dummy pronoun *it* in subject position and the clausal argument in clause-final position, and

[THAT DANA IS HERE] IS OBVIOUS $\longleftrightarrow$
It is obvious that Dana is here.

[FOR JO TO CRY] WOULD UPSET LOU $\longleftrightarrow$
It would upset Lou for Jo to cry.

It is well-documented that extraposed clauses do not function as subjects, and do not have the factive (presupposed) character of clausal subjects (Morgan 1975, Horn 1986).

Q: Why did you stay home on Monday?
A: It's obvious that I thought it was Sunday.
(A: !That I thought it was Sunday is obvious.)

For some speakers, gerunds can be extraposed:

[SWIMMING IN THE NUDE] IS FUN $\longleftrightarrow$
It's fun swimming in the nude.

The transformational rule of Extraposition was sometimes claimed to be obligatory for certain verbs, such as *seem*, and *occur*, on the basis of such pairs of sentences as:

*That Dana is innocent seems.
It seems that Dana is innocent.

*That Dana might leave occurred to Lou.
It occurred to Lou that Dana might leave.

In fact, many of these verbs permit Raising into Subject position as an alternative (cf. *Dana seems to be innocent*), and others can be found unextraposed, e.g.,

That Smith could have locked the house from inside and climbed out the open window occurred to only one of the jurors.

That they could have gone to Paris, picked up the packages, and flown right home again never occurred to us.

Similar facts obtain for quite a few western European languages.

A clause is never extraposed beyond the boundaries of the clause of which it is the logical subject. Structure (1) below might have a surface structure like (2): *That it surprised you that Dana admired Lou is obvious*, but never one like *That it surprised you is obvious that Dana admired Lou*, which would have a structure like (3).

It has been claimed that object clauses as well as subject clauses may be extraposed, as in *I resent it that/when he never calls me*, but whether the *it* that occurs in such sentences is evidence of Extraposition is open to question.

(1)

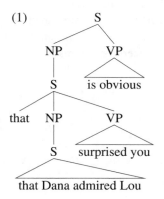

(2)

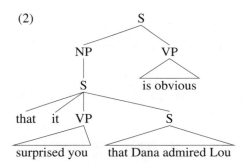

(3)

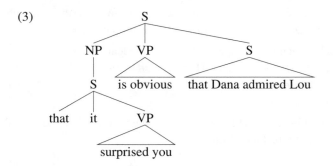

References and complications: Rosenbaum 1967, Ross 1967/83, Morgan 1968, 1975; Kiparsky and Kiparsky 1970, Jacobson and Neubauer 1974, Green and Morgan 1976, Chomsky 1977, Horn 1986.

16. Sentence-raising (or S-Lifting, Slifting). Optional, governed.

Finite clauses that are the object complement of verbs referring to speech and belief (i.e., *think, seems, bet, guess, promise, say, suppose*, and many others), may appear preposed and complementizerless, Chomsky-adjoined to the rest of their clause.

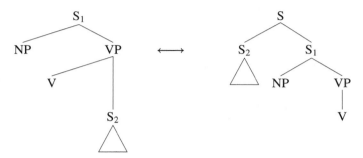

I THINK SOY SAUCE IS GOOD FOR YOU $\longleftrightarrow$
Soy sauce is good for you, I think. (*That soy sauce is good for you, I think.)

IT SEEMS (THAT) DANA IS INNOCENT $\longleftrightarrow$ (*That) Dana is innocent, it seems.

SUE SAYS DANA IS NO ORDINARY FOOL $\longleftrightarrow$ Dana is no ordinary fool, Sue says.

Slifting makes the logical matrix clause pragmatically transparent, and gives the logical complement an independent illocutionary force, to the point where it permits the syntactic trappings of main clauses with that force.

Harry has been named Hogwarts champion, he learns.
Harry learns he has been named Hogwarts champion.
Where is it, I wonder.
Put it over there, I guess.

This rule is found in many languages, but in some it is restricted to a smaller class of governing verbs than in English.

References and complications: Ross 1973, Green 1975, 1976.

17. Niching. Optional, ungoverned?

Parenthetical phrases, including sentence adverbials like *frankly* or *obviously,* and the main clause remnant defined by S-Lifting, may appear at certain points within the clauses they are predicated of.

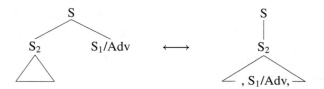

GUPPIES TASTE BETTER WITH SALT, I THINK
⟷ Guppies taste better, I think, with salt.
Or: ⟷ Guppies, I think, taste better with salt.

References and complications: Ross 1973, Corum 1975.

Some Complementizer Phenomena

18. *That*-deletion in complement clauses. Optional, governed.
 If a *that*-clause is not in clause-initial position, the *that* may be absent when the clause is the complement of certain verbs and adjectives (e.g., *think, regret, obvious, clear* but not *snicker, frustrating, annoying*).

IT'S CLEAR THAT CHRIS SHOULD DO IT ⟷
It's clear Chris should do it.

JAMIE DENIED THAT SAM WAS DRUGGED ⟷
Jamie denied Sam was drugged.

THAT CHRIS WAS A BROWN BAGGER IS CLEAR ←X→
*Chris was a brown bagger is clear.

CHRIS SNICKERED THAT HE HAD NEVER HEARD SUCH A SILLY DOG ←X→
*Chris snickered he had never heard such a silly dog.

THAT SANDY WAS GIVEN SPECIAL PRIVILEGES, JAMIE DOUBTED
←X→ *Sandy was given special privileges, Jamie doubted.

References and complications: Bolinger 1972, Stowell 1981, Rizzi 1990.

19. *To*-deletion. Obligatory, governed.
 Infinitives that are the complement of a small set of verbs including *make, let, help* and *have* appear without the complementizer *to*. This *to* is absent in

certain contexts (generally where the verb is uninflected) for complements of
dare and *need*. In passive structures the *to* must generally be present.

I MADE BOHUMIL TO DEFACE A SCULPTURE ⟷
I made Bohumil deface a sculpture.

I FORCED BOHUMIL TO DEFACE A SCULPTURE ←X→
*I forced Bohumil deface a sculpture.

I need to translate.
*I need translate.
*Need I to translate?
Need/Dare I translate?
Do I need/dare to translate?
I need/dare not translate.
He need not translate
*He needs not translate

Chris made Lou leave.
*Lou was made leave.
Lou was made to leave.

Chris let the ball drop/fall.
The ball was let drop/fall.
*The ball was let to drop.
Lou let the prisoner escape.
*The prisoner was let escape.
*The prisoner was let to escape.

20. *For*-deletion. Obligatory, ungoverned.

In transformational accounts where infinitives were generated via deletion
of a NP that followed the infinitive clause complementizer *for*, deletion of *for*
was seen as obligatory in most dialects of modern English.

CHRIS$_i$ WANTS [FOR CHRIS$_i$ TO LEAVE] ⟷ CHRIS WANTS [FOR
TO LEAVE] ⟷ Chris wants to leave.

References and complications: Rosenbaum 1967, Sag 1997.

21. Preposition deletion. Obligatory, ungoverned.

Prepositions that occur with verbs and adjectives which allow a propositional object complement (e.g., *afraid of, annoyed at, decide on*) must be

absent if the verb or adjective is followed immediately by a finite or infinitival clause. Otherwise, the preposition shows up.

> I'M AFRAID OF (THAT) MY NOSE IS PEELING ⟷
> I'm afraid (that) my nose is peeling.

But: I'm afraid of war.)
      What I am afraid of is that my nose is peeling.

> I WAS ANNOYED AT TO FIND HIM HERE ⟷ I was annoyed to find him here.

> I PERSUADED HIM OF (THAT) HE SHOULD LEAVE ⟷
> I persuaded him (that) he should leave.

> THEY DECIDED ON TO LEAVE ⟷ They decided to leave.

References and complications: Rosenbaum 1967.

Other Reordering Constructions

22. Extraposition from NP. Optional, ungoverned.
    A structure containing a NP with a phrasal or clausal postmodifier (e.g., a relative clause) may appear with the postmodifier at the end of the clause containing the NP:

> A MAN [WHO HAS 3 EARS] JUST CAME IN ⟷
> A man just came in who has 3 ears.

> THE CLAIM [THAT ZINJANTHROPUS COULD DO CALCULUS]
> HAS BEEN CIRCULATING
> ⟷ The claim has been circulating that Zinjanthropus could do calculus.

> AN ANALYSIS [OF THE CONTRIBUTION OF WRITING ACTIVI-
> TIES TO THE ACQUISITION OF READING SKILLS] WILL BE PRE-
> SENTED
> ⟷ An analysis will be presented of the contribution of writing activities to the acquisition of reading skills.

I DON'T KNOW HOW THE RANGE [OF ALTERNATIVES TO
CHOOSE FROM] ARISES
⟶ I don't know how the range arises of alternatives to choose from.

For many speakers, this construction is unacceptable if an extraposed modifier occurs in a position where it could have originated in the first place; that is, if it could be interpreted as modifying the NP that immediately precedes it. For these speakers, THE ARTIST WHO TAUGHT THAT CLASS NOMINATED THE DESIGNER cannot be related to *The artist nominated the designer who taught that class*, but A WOMAN WHO WAS PREGNANT KISSED MY BROTHER can be related to *A woman kissed my brother who was pregnant*. For other speakers, sentences with Extraposition from NP are unacceptable if the extraposed phrase would be unacceptable as a modifier of the NP immediately preceding it, even if they would be unambiguous. For them, A GUY WHO LIKES MOZART WANTED TO DATE THREE DISCO DANCERS cannot be related by Extraposition from NP to *A guy wanted to date three disco dancers who likes Mozart* because *three disco dancers who likes Mozart* is unacceptable as an NP. It may be that this judgement is an artifact of the data-gathering context, however, and not a question of competence.

This construction has been observed to allow the content of the relative clause to function as asserted.

A: A man came in who was in "Cats" on Broadway.
B: No, he wasn't!

References and complications: Ziv, 1975, 1976; Lakoff 1972; Hayes 1976a, Stucky 1987.

23. Adverb preposing. Optional, ungoverned.
Clausal and phrasal adverbs may appear in clause-initial position.

I FOUND A ROBIN IN THE GARDEN/WHEN I LOOKED OUT THE
WINDOW ⟶
In the garden,/When I looked out the window, I found a robin.

Ordinarily, adverbs appear no farther to the "left" or "up" than the beginning of their own clause:

I SAID THAT I'LL LEAVE IN 10 MINUTES ⟷
I said that, in 10 minutes, I'll leave.

I SAID THAT I'LL LEAVE IN 10 MINUTES ←X→
∗In 10 minutes, I said that I'll leave.

But under certain conditions they may occur at the head of higher clauses:

> I HOPE YOU'LL VISIT THE GARDEN BEFORE YOU LEAVE
> ⟷ I hope that before you leave, you'll visit the garden.
> OR: ⟷ Before you leave, I hope you'll visit the garden.

References and complications: Ross 1967/83, Davison 1970, Pollard and Sag 1994.

24. Topicalization (Y(iddish)-movement). Optional, ungoverned.
    A constituent may appear in clause-initial position instead of in its normal position. Restrictions vary greatly from dialect to dialect.

I DON'T LIKE CANNED SPINACH ⟷ Canned spinach, I don't like.

I LIKE THAT ⟷ That I like.

Area contractors are waiting for their phones to ring, and ring they will, when rooftop snow begins to melt later this week.

Cases like the following are not acceptable in some dialects, although people from New York City and environs find them perfectly natural. Speakers in areas where Yiddish-influenced English is spoken may employ this construction in a wider range of syntactic structures.

> HE ISN'T ABLE TO LEAP TALL BUILDINGS AT A SINGLE BOUND
> ⟷ Able to leap tall buildings at a single bound, he isn't.

Topicalization allows a constituent to appear indefinitely far away from the clause it is semantically bound to.

> I THINK THAT BOB SAID DALE HEARD SAM LIKES CUCUMBERS
> ⟷ Cucumbers, I think that Bob said Dale heard Sam likes.

Pragmatically, there are actually two or three distinct constructions which share this gross syntax. They differ in their prosody as well as their discourse presuppositions. Constructions with similar syntactic properties are found in many languages.

References and complications: Ross 1967/83, 1969c; Prince 1981, 1984; Olsen 1986; Ward 1983, 1985/1988, 1990,; Birner and Ward 1998.

25. Left dislocation. Optional, ungoverned.

An NP may appear in clause-initial position, instead of in its normal position, where a pronoun with the corresponding person, number, and gender, and corresponding case appears.

> THE WOMAN YOUR LAWYER SUBPOENAED IS GOING
> TO TELL THE JURY THAT THE DEFENDANT WITH THE
> TATTOO HAD BEEN DRINKING
> ⟵⟶ The woman your lawyer subpoenaed, he is going to tell the
> jury that the defendant with the tattoo had been drinking.

> Or: ⟵⟶ The jury, the woman your lawyer subpoenaed is going to
> tell them that the defendant with the tattoo had been drinking.

The dependency between the initial NP and the matching pronoun is unbounded.

> The defendant with the tattoo, the woman your lawyer subpoenaed is
> going to tell the jury he'd been drinking.

References and complications: Ross, 1967/83, Prince 1984.

26. Cleft. Optional, ungoverned.

Corresponding to any non-inverted grammatical declarative sentence, there is a sentence with expletive *it* as the subject and *be* as the main verb, where a focussed phrase (usually an NP or a PP or other adverbial modifier) is the complement of *be*, and *be* is followed by *that* or an appropriate relative pronoun and the rest of the corresponding declarative sentence, minus the focussed phrase.

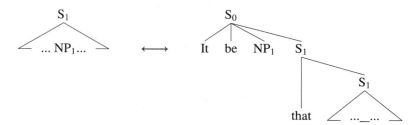

(This construction is much easier to produce than to describe—like most constructions.)

LOU SAW CHRIS YESTERDAY ⟷ It was Lou who/that saw Chris yesterday.
Or: ⟷ It was Chris who/that Lou saw yesterday.
Or: ⟷ It was yesterday that/?when Lou saw Chris.

THEY GAVE THE MUGGER MONEY BECAUSE HE HAD A KNIFE ⟷ It was because he had a knife that they gave the mugger money.

References and complications: Akmajian 1978; McCawley 1978b, Prince 1978, Delahunty 1981, Gazdar et al., 1985.

27. Pseudo-cleft. Optional, ungoverned.

Corresponding to any non-inverted grammatical declarative sentence, there is a sentence where a focussed phrase (usually an NP or a PP or other adverbial modifier) is the complement of *be*, the subject is an embedded question beginning with the interrogative pronoun corresponding to the singled-out phrase, and the focussed phrase is followed by the corresponding declarative structure, minus what corresponds to the focussed phrase.

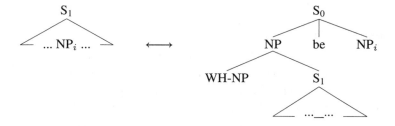

The pseudo-cleft construction is ordinarily unacceptable if the focussed NP refers to a human being:

> I SAW A DOG ⟷ What I saw was a dog.

> CHRIS THINKS THAT IT'S RAINING ⟷
> What Chris thinks is that it's raining.

> THE D9 RAN OVER MY BOW-TIE ⟷
> What ran over my bow-tie was the D9.

> CHRIS LOVES SANDY ⟷ *Who/*What Chris loves is Sandy.

But compare:

> CHRIS SAW DALE ⟷ What/*Who Chris saw was Dale.

> CHRIS NEEDS TO CONSULT WITH A LINGUIST ⟷
> What/*Who Chris needs to consult with is a linguist.

> CHRIS LOVES HIMSELF ⟷ What/*Who Chris loves is himself.

In some analyses, pseudo-cleft structures are related to other structures via cleft structures. Many speakers find pseudo-clefted adverbs unacceptable unless they are inverted with the *be* (see pages 126–127, item 8).

> CHRIS LEFT YESTERDAY ⟷ WHEN CHRIS LEFT WAS YESTER-
> DAY ⟷ Yesterday was when Chris left.

References and complications: Akmajian 1978, Higgins 1978, Prince 1978, Lasnik and Saito 1992.

Conjunction Phenomena

28. Conjunction reduction. Optional? ungoverned.

Two or more constituents of the same category may be coordinated and function as a single grammatical unit. In the early days of transformational grammar, it was assumed that coordinate phrases arose from the reduction of coordinate clauses that were identical except for one constituent.

DALE LIKE POTATOES AND HARRY LIKE POTATOES ⟷
Dale and Harry like potatoes.

BARBARA KISSED CHRIS OR BARBARA HUGGED CHRIS ⟷
Barbara kissed or hugged Chris.

WE LIKE TURNIPS BUT WE HATE RUTABAGAS ⟷
We like turnips but hate rutabagas.

The exact definition of "same category" is elusive. Verbs of different tenses can be coordinated, as can nouns of different person, number, and gender (but generally not case, unless the instances of the distinct cases have the same morphology). Predicate phrases with distinct sorts of heads can even be conjoined.

Jordan was and is the best player of all time.
She and her brothers all qualified for the tournament.
Dale is at home in North Dakota and glad to be alive.

But prepositional phrases with different functions sound pretty bad conjoined, and cannot be reduced even if headed by the same preposition.

??Chris arrived on a motorcycle and on time.
∗ Chris arrived on a motorcycle and time.

How a single transformational rule could be written to do this was never clear. In addition, there are coordinate structures where one of the apparent conjuncts does not constitute a phrase in other environments; Hankamer (1971) gives the name *Stripping* to cases where a negative adverb and unlike "remainder" follow a full clause:

WE LIKE TURNIPS BUT WE DON'T LIKE RUTABAGAS ⟷
We like turnips, but not rutabagas.

GWENDOLYN SMOKES MARIJUANA, BUT GWENDOLYN
SELDOM SMOKES MARIJUANA IN HER OWN APARTMENT ⟷
Gwendolyn smokes marijuana, but seldom in her own apartment.

ALAN LIKES TO SWIM, BUT SANDY DOES NOT LIKE TO SWIM
⟵⟶ Alan likes to swim, but not Sandy.

Not all conjoined constituents can be analyzed in terms of conjoined sentences:

Chris and Pat are a cute couple. ←X→
CHRIS IS A CUTE COUPLE AND PAT IS A CUTE COUPLE

Jadeite and nephrite are similar. ←X→
JADEITE IS SIMILAR AND NEPHRITE IS SIMILAR

References and complications: Ross 1967/83, articles in Reibel and Schane (71–142), Dougherty 1970, 1971; Hankamer 1971, Gazdar 1981; Sag, Gazdar, Wasow, and Weisler 1985.

29. Gapping. Optional, ungoverned.
All but two or more major constituents of a sentence may be absent if identical to corresponding parts of a coordinate sentence.

KIM ORDERED POTATOES AND DANA ORDERED BEANS ⟵⟶
Kim ordered potatoes and Dana beans.

SARA GAVE A NICKEL TO DALE AND SAM GAVE A DIME TO SUE ⟵⟶ Sara gave a nickel to Dale and Sam a dime to Sue.

DALE ASKED LOU TO LEAVE AND SAM ASKED SUE TO DANCE
←X→ *Dale asked Lou to leave and Sam Sue to dance.

DALE ASKED IF LOU WOULD LEAVE AND SAM ASKED IF SUE WOULD DANCE
⟵⟶ Dale asked if Lou would leave and Sam if Sue would dance.

In English, Gapping is always "forwards:" gaps have an antecedent in a preceding clause. In other languages, it may be "backwards," with the first clause containing the gap.

References and complications: Ross 1970, Dingwall 1969, Hankamer 1973a, Jake 1977, Levin 1986, Sag, Gazdar, Wasow and Weisler 1985, Johnson 1991, Lasnik 1999.

30. Non-constituent coordination. Ungoverned.

Sometimes parallel sequences that are not constituents are linked by a coordinating conjunction.

> Chris gave Kim a bell, Lou a book, and Jo a candle.
> The group asked the council for a permit and the senator for a donation.
> The group persuaded the senator to resign and the governor to postpone making an appointment.

References and complications: Dowty 1988.

31. Right-node raising. Optional, ungoverned.

Parallel clauses missing a rightmost constituent can be conjoined, with a phrase satisfying the subcategorization requirements of both clauses Chomsky-adjoined to the right of the coordinate structure.

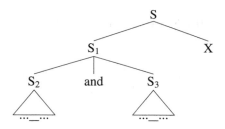

> Dale picked, Lou peeled, and Harry cooked the potatoes.
> It's possible, and it ought to be easy to verify, that Bonnie left.
> Dale signed the transmittal form, and Lou witnessed it, yesterday.
> Chris sent a bouquet to, and Dale actually met, one of the Rock Bottom Remainders.

References and complications: Postal 1974, Gazdar 1981, McCawley 1982, Levine 1985.

32. Verb phrase deletion. Optional, ungoverned.

If a phrase-marker contains a VP which is identical to a VP in prior discourse, a sub-constituent of the VP may be absent, as long as at least one verbal element remains.

CHRIS MAY HAVE BEEN WATCHING TV, AND MARIA
MAY HAVE BEEN WATCHING TV TOO
⟷ Chris may have been watching TV, and Maria may have
been too.

Or: ⟷ Chris may have been watching TV, and Maria may have
too.

Or: ⟷ Chris may have been watching TV, and Maria may too.

IF YOU WILL BE STUDYING, I WILL BE STUDYING
⟷ If you will be studying, I will be.

Or: ⟷ If you will be studying, I will.

But: ←X→ *If you will be studying, I.

Some speakers find this construction unacceptable if a missing constituent has
a different stem of a suppletive verb from its antecedent.

SINCE WILT IS TALL, HIS SON WILL BE TALL ←X→
*Since Wilt is tall, his son will.

SINCE CHRIS WENT TO PARIS, I WILL GO TO PARIS ⟷
%Since Chris went to Paris, I will.

But:

SINCE CHRIS ATE SOME OF THE SOUP, I WILL EAT SOME OF
THE SOUP ⟷
Since Chris ate some of the soup, I will.

References and complications: Grinder and Postal 1971, Hankamer and Sag
1976, Sag 1977, Lappin 1996.

Other Deletion Rules

33. Discourse Deletions.

The conditions for Stripping, Gapping, VP-deletion, Sentence Pronominalization, Sluicing, Conjunction Reduction, and no doubt other deletion
constructions, as well as ordinary definite and indefinite pronominalization
may be met in sentences adjacent in a discourse, even in utterances of different
speakers:

Stripping	Joe: Gwen smokes marijuana. Moe: But never on Sundays.
Gapping	Pam: Lou gave Dale a nickel. Sam: And Harriet a quarter.
VP-deletion	Ann: Will you vote for Paley? Jan: Yes, if you will.
Sentence pronominalization	Fred: Your tie is crooked. Ned: I know it.
Sluicing	Ed: Lou gave someone a nickel. Ted: I wonder who.
Conjunction reduction	Beth: Lou gave Dale a nickel. Seth: And a copy of *Linguistic Inquiry*.
Indefinite pronominalization	Dan: My dad bought a half-ton pickup. Jan: Well, my dad bought one with a king cab.
Definite pronominalization	Sean: A thief broke Chris's arm. Dawn: Was he arrested?

This means that a grammar which purported to describe these constructions by means of transformational rules would have to have rules which referred to discourse contexts. A non-transformational account would simply have to predict that the structures were well-formed (or support auxiliary hypotheses which predicted the circumstances in which ill-formed structures would be judged acceptable).

References and complications: Morgan 1973, Hankamer and Sag 1976, Lappin 1996.

34. Comparative deletion. Ungoverned, obligatory.

Comparative constructions are licensed by a comparative quantifier (*more, less, as*) which selects a complementizer (*than* or *as*) whose object is a phrase or non-constituent clause remnant (e.g., a clause lacking an object). The complement is interpreted as a clause with an indefinite quantifier whose missing parts are reconstructed from what is present in the clause containing the comparative quantifier.

I solved more problems than Lou (solved). ⟷
I SOLVED [MORE THAN LOU SOLVED Quant PROBLEMS]$_Q$
PROBLEMS

He likes Kim more than (he likes) Chris. ⟷
HE LIKES KIM MORE THAN HE LIKES CHRIS Quant MUCH

He likes Kim more than Chris (likes Kim). ⟷
HE LIKES KIM MORE THAN CHRIS LIKES KIM Quant MUCH

The dependency licensed by this construction is unbounded.

Kim knows more people than Chris said we could ever hope to meet _.

Morgan (1973) observed that the most minimal comparative forms permit hyperbolic interpretations, while less minimal forms allow only literal readings:

Hans leaps like a gazelle.
Hans leaps like a gazelle does.

References and complications: Bresnan 1973, 1975, 1977; Morgan 1973; Hankamer 1973b; Sag 1977, Pinkham 1982.

35. Comparative subdeletion. Ungoverned, obligatory.

This structure is similar to the comparative construction, except that it is only a quantifier that is missing and has to be reconstructed, not a phrase containing a quantified expression. The missing quantifier must be of the same type as the explicit quantifier.

There were more men on that show than there were _ women. ⟷
THERE WERE [MORE THAN THERE WERE Quant MANY
WOMEN]$_Q$ MEN ON THAT SHOW

There was as much rice as there was jello. ⟷
THERE WAS [AS MUCH AS THERE WAS Quant MUCH
JELLO]$_Q$ RICE .

*There was more rice than there were women.

This dependency is also unbounded.

> They are going to hire more women than anyone ever thought the management would agree to allow them to hire _ men.

References and complications: Bresnan 1973, 1975, 1977.

Non-Clausemate Reflexive Rules

36. Reflexivization in *picture*-NPs. Optional, ungoverned.

A noun phrase in the complement of a "picture-word" like *picture, story, description, joke*, etc. may appear as a reflexive pronoun if it corresponds in person, number, and gender to a discourse antecedent.

The reflexive may precede and command the antecedent:

> The picture of himself$_i$ that Chris$_i$ said was in the Post Office was taken in 1973.
> That picture of himself$_i$ embarrasses Chris$_i$.

The dependency between the reflexive and any antecedent is unbounded.

> CHRIS$_i$ SAID THAT IT WAS POSSIBLE THAT THERE WAS A PICTURE OF CHRIS$_i$ IN THE POST OFFICE. $\longleftrightarrow$
> Chris said that it was possible that there was a picture of himself in the Post Office.

The dependency may be discourse-licensed.

> The twins were thinking about a gift for their parents. A picture of themselves seemed like a good idea.

References and complications: Ross 1970, Jackendoff 1972, Zribi-Hertz 1989, Chomsky 1991, Reinhart and Reuland 1993, Pollard and Sag 1994, Huang and Liu 2000.

37. Reflexivization in *as for NP* phrases. Optional, ungoverned.

The NP object of *as for* may appear as the appropriate reflexive pronoun if it has a discourse antecedent.

> Chris$_i$ realized that as for himself$_i$ there was no chance of winning.

A syntactic antecedent (one in the same sentence) must be a subject.

Chris told Dale$_i$ that as for *herself$_i$/her$_i$, she$_i$ could never win.

References and complications: Ross 1970, Zribi-Hertz 1989.

38. Reflexivization in *like NP* phrases. Optional, ungoverned.

An NP which occurs as the object of a postmodifying prepositional phrase introduced by the preposition *like* may be a reflexive pronoun. It may have the same reference as a discourse antecedent, or have a syntactic antecedent which precedes and commands.

Jane$_i$ said that Max heard from Harry that the AEC said that physicists like herself$_i$/her$_i$ would be taxed at a lower rate.

A woman who admires physicists like him$_i$/*himself$_i$ told Albert$_i$ about some AEC plot.

The controller needn't be a subject:

Albert told Jane$_i$ that physicists like herself$_i$ were being overworked.

References and complications: Ross 1970.

39. Reflexivization in coordinate agent phrases. Optional, ungoverned.

When the *by NP* agent phrase in a passive verb phrase contains as prepositional object a coordinate NP whose second member has a commanding coreferent in the sentence, the object may appear as the corresponding reflexive pronoun.

Joe$_i$ claimed that no one realized that the paper would have to be written by Ann and himself$_i$.

That the paper would have to be written by Ann and himself$_i$ was obvious to Joe$_i$.

When the controller doesn't command the reflexive, such sentences are less than acceptable.

?*A woman who knows Tom$_i$ well says that the paper was written by Ann and himself$_i$.

References and complications: Ross 1970.

REFERENCES

Aissen, Judith. 1975. Presentational *there* Insertion; A Cyclic Root Transformation. *Papers from the Eleventh Regional Meeting, Chicago Linguistic Society*, 11:1–14. Chicago: Chicago Linguistic Society.

Akmajian, Adrian. 1978. *Aspects of the Grammar of Focus in English*. New York: Garland.

Akmajian, Adrian, and Frank Heny. 1975. *Introduction to the Principles of Transformational Syntax*. Cambridge, MA: MIT Press.

Akmajian, Adrian, and Thomas Wasow. 1975. The Constituent Structure of VP and AUX and the Position of the Verb *be*. *Linguistic Analysis* 1;3.

Andrews, Avery D. 1971. Understood Tense and Underlying Forms. *Linguistic Inquiry* 2:542–543.

Bach, Emmon. 1971. Questions. *Linguistic Inquiry* 2:153–166.

Bach, Emmon. 1974. *Syntactic Theory*. New York: Holt, Rinehart and Winston.

Bach, Emmon. 1982. Purpose Clauses and Control. *The Nature of Syntactic Representation*, ed. by P. Jacobsen and G. Pullum, 35–58. Dordrecht: Reidel.

Baker, Carl Leroy. 1968. Indirect Questions in English. University of Illinois dissertation.

Baker, Carl Leroy. 1970a. Notes on the Description of English Questions; the role of an abstract question morpheme. *Foundations of Language* 6:197–219.

Baker, Carl Leroy. 1970b. Double Negatives. *Linguistic Inquiry* 1:169–186.

Baker, Carl Leroy, and Michael Brame. 1972. 'Global Rules': A Rejoinder. *Language* 48:51–75.

Banfield, Ann. 1973. Narrative Style and the Grammar of Direct and Indirect Speech. *Foundations of Language* 10:1–39.

Baxter, David. 1999. English Goal Infinitives. Ph.D. dissertation, University of Illinois. Urbana, Illinois.

Berman, Arlene. 1973. A Constraint on *tough*-movement. *Papers from the Ninth Regional Meeting, Chicago Linguistic Society*, edited by Claudia Corum, T. Cedric Smith-Stark, and Ann Weiser, 34–43. Chicago: Chicago Linguistic Society.

Berman, Arlene. 1974a. On the VSO Hypothesis. *Linguistic Inquiry* 5:1-38.

Berman, Arlene. 1974b. Tripl-*ing*. *Linguistic Inquiry* 4:401–403.

Berman, Arlene. 1974c. Infinitival Relative Constructions. *Papers from the Tenth Regional Meeting, Chicago Linguistic Society*, 37–46. Chicago: Chicago Linguistic Society.

173

Berman, Arlene, and Susan Schmerling. 1973. Syntax Bibliography. Dittoed. University of Texas at Austin.

Birner, Betty J. 1992. The Discourse Function of Inversion in English. Ph.D. dissertation. Evanston: Northwestern University.

Birner, Betty J. 1994. Information status and word order: an analysis of English inversion. *Language* 70: 233–259.

Birner, Betty J., and Gregory Ward. 1998. Information status and noncanonical word order in English. Amsterdam/Philadelphia: John Benjamins.

Blake, Barry J. 1990. *Relational Grammar*. London: Routledge.

Bolinger, Dwight. 1967. The Imperative in English. *To Honor Roman Jakobson*, I. The Hague: Mouton.

Bolinger, Dwight. 1971. *The Phrasal Verb in English*. Cambridge: Harvard University Press.

Bolinger, Dwight. 1972. *That's that*. The Hague: Mouton.

Bolinger, Dwight. 1977. *Meaning and Form*. London: Longmans.

Borer, Hagit. 1981. *Parametric variation in clitic constructions*. Ph.D. diss, MIT.

Borkin, Ann. 1971. *Where the Rules Fail: A Student's Guide*. Ann Arbor: Department of Linguistics, University of Michigan. (Reproduced by Indiana University Linguistics Club)

Borkin, Ann. 1972. Coreference and Beheaded NPs. *Papers in Linguistics* 5: 28-45.

Borkin, Ann. 1974. Raising to Object Position. University of Michigan dissertation.

Borsley, Robert, and Kersti Borjars, eds. To appear. *Non-transformational Syntax: A Guide to Current Models*. Oxford: Blackwell.

Bransford, John D., and M. K. Johnson. 1973. Consideration of Some Problems in Comprehension. *Visual Information Processing*, ed. by W. G. Chase. New York: Academic Press.

Bresnan, Joan. 1972. The Theory of Complementation in English Syntax. MIT Ph.D. diss. (Published in 1978; New York: Garland)

Bresnan, Joan. 1973. Syntax of the Comparative Clause Construction in English. *Linguistic Inquiry* 4: 275–343.

Bresnan, Joan. 1975. Comparative Deletion and Constraints on Transformations. *Linguistic Analysis* 1: 25–74.

Bresnan, Joan. 1977. Variables in the Theory of Transformations. *Formal Syntax*, ed. by P. Culicover, T. Wasow, and A. Akmajian, 157–196. New York: Academic Press.

Bresnan, Joan. 1978. A Realistic Transformational Grammar. *Linguistic Theory and Psychological Reality*, ed. by M. Halle et al., 1–59. Cambridge, MA: MIT Press.

Bresnan, Joan. 1982a. *The Mental Representation of Grammatical Relations*. Cambridge, MA: MIT Press.

Bresnan, Joan. 1982b. Control and Complementation. In Bresnan 1982a, 282–390.

Burt, Marina K. 1970. *From Deep to Surface Structure*. New York: Harper and Row.

Chomsky, Noam. 1955. *The Logical Structure of Linguistic Theory*. Published 1975, New York: Plenum.

Chomsky, Noam. 1957. *Syntactic Structures*. The Hague: Mouton.

Chomsky, Noam. 1964. The Logical Basis of Linguistic Theory. *Proceedings of the Ninth International Congress of Linguists*, ed. by H. Lunt. The Hague: Mouton.

Chomsky, Noam. 1965. *Aspects of the Theory of Syntax*. Cambridge, MA: MIT Press.

Chomsky, Noam. 1969. Remarks on Nominalization. *Readings in English Transformational Grammar*, ed. by Roderick Jacobs and P. S. Rosenbaum, 184–221. Waltham, MA: Ginn.

Chomsky, Noam. 1971. Deep Structure, Surface Structure, and Semantic Interpretation. *Semantics, an Interdisciplinary Reader*, ed. by Danny Steinberg and L. Jakobovits, 183–216. Cambridge: Cambridge University Press.

Chomsky, Noam. 1973. Conditions on Transformations. *Festschrift for Morris Halle*, ed. by S. Anderson and P. Kiparsky, 232–286. New York: Holt, Rinehart, and Winston.

Chomsky, Noam. 1975. *Reflections on Language*. New York: Pantheon.

Chomsky, Noam. 1977. On Wh-movement. *Formal Syntax*, ed. by P. Culicover, A. Akmajian, and T. Wasow, 71–132. New York: Academic Press.

Chomsky, Noam. 1980. On Binding. *Linguistic Inquiry* 11: 1–46.

Chomsky, Noam. 1981. *Lectures on Government and Binding*. Dordrecht: Foris.

Chomsky, Noam. 1982. *Some Concepts and Consequences of the Theory of Government and Binding*. Cambridge, MA: MIT Press.

Chomsky, Noam. 1986. *Knowledge of Language: Its Nature, Origins, and Use*. New York: Praeger.

Chomsky, Noam. 1991. Some Notes on Economy of Derivation and Representation. *Principles and Parameters in Comparative Grammar*, edited by Robert Freidin, 417-454. Cambridge, MA: MIT Press.

Chomsky, Noam. 1995. *The Minimalist Program*. Cambridge, MA: MIT Press.

Chomsky, Noam, and Howard Lasnik. 1977. Filters and Control. *Linguistic Inquiry* 8: 425–504.

Cole, Peter. and Jerry Morgan. 1975. *Syntax and Semantics, Vol. 3: Speech Acts*. New York: Academic Press.

Comrie, Bernard. 1977. In Defense of Spontaneous Demotion. *Syntax and Semantics, Vol. 8: Grammatical Relations*, ed. by P. Cole and J. Sadock, 47–58. New York: Academic Press.

Corum, Claudia. 1975. A Pragmatic Analysis of Parenthetical Adjuncts. *Papers from the Eleventh Regional Meeting, Chicago Linguistic Society*, 133–141. Chicago: Chicago Linguistic Society,

Cote, Sharon. 1996. Grammatical and Discourse Properties of Null Arguments in English. Ph.D. dissertation, University of Pennsylvania. Philadelphia, PA.

Davis, Anthony, and Jean-Pierre Koenig. 2000. Linking as constraints on word classes in a hierarchical lexicon. *Language* 76: 56–91.

Davison, Alice. 1970. Causal Adverbs and Performative Verbs. *Papers from the Sixth Regional Meeting*, Chicago Linguistic Society, 190–201. Chicago: Chicago Linguistic Society.

Davison, Alice. 1980. Peculiar Passives. *Language* 56:42–66.

Delahunty, Gerald P. 1981. Topics in the Syntax and Semantics of English Cleft Sentences. Ph.D. diss. University of California at Irvine.

Dingwall, William. 1969. Secondary Conjunction and Universal Grammar. *Papers in Linguistics*, 1: 207–230.

Dougherty, Ray. 1970. A Grammar of Coordinate Conjoined Structures, I. *Language* 46: 850–898.

Dougherty, Ray. 1971. A Grammar of Coordinate Conjoined Structures, II. *Language* 47: 298–339.

Dowty, David. 1982. Grammatical Relations and Montague Grammar. *The Nature of Syntactic Representation*, ed. by P. Jacobson and G. Pullum, 79–130. Dordrecht: Reidel.

Dowty, David. 1988. Type Raising, Functional Composition, and Non-constituent Coordination. *Categorial Grammars and Natural Language Structures*, edited by Richard Oehrle, Emmon Bach, and D. Wheeler, 153–198. Dordrecht: D. Reidel.

Dowty, David, Robert Wall, and Stanley Peters. 1981. *An Introduction to Montague Semantics*. Dordrecht: Reidel.

Emonds, Joseph. 1970/1976. *A Transformational Approach to English Syntax*. New York: Academic Press.

Fillmore, Charles. 1963. The Position of Embedding Transformations in a Grammar. *Word* 19: 208–231.

Fillmore, Charles. 1965. *Indirect Object Constructions in English and the Ordering of Transformations*. The Hague: Mouton.

Flickinger, Daniel. 1983. Lexical Heads and Phrasal Gaps. *Proceedings of the 2nd West Coast Conference on Formal Linguistics*, ed. by M. Barlow, D. Flickinger, and M. Wescoat, 89–101. Stanford, Ca.: Stanford Linguistics Association.

Fodor, Janet D. 1974. Like-subject Verbs and Causal Clauses in English. *Journal of Linguistics* 10: 95–110.

Fraser, Bruce. 1973. The Verb-Particle Combination in English. Tokyo: Taishukan.

Gazdar, Gerald. 1981. Unbounded Dependencies and Coordinate Structure. *Linguistic Inquiry* 12: 155–184.

Gazdar, Gerald. 1982. Phrase Structure Grammar. *The Nature of Syntactic Representation*, ed. by P. Jacobson and G. Pullum, 131–186. Dordrecht: Reidel.

Gazdar, Gerald, Ewan Klein, and Geoffrey Pullum. 1978. *A Bibliography of Contemporary Linguistic Research*. New York: Garland.

Gazdar, Gerald, Ewan Klein, Geoffrey Pullum, and Ivan Sag. 1982. Coordinate Structures and Unbounded Dependencies. *Developments in Generalized Phrase Structure Grammar*, ed. by M. Barlow, D. Flickinger, and I. Sag, 38–68. Indiana University Linguistic Club.

Gazdar, Gerald, Ewan Klein, Geoffrey Pullum, and Ivan Sag. 1985. *Generalized Phrase Structure Grammar*. Cambridge, MA: Harvard University Press.

Gazdar, Gerald, and Geoffrey Pullum. 1982. Generalized Phrase Structure Grammar: A Theoretical Synopsis. Indiana University Linguistics Club.

Gazdar, Gerald, Geoffrey Pullum, and Ivan Sag. 1982. Auxiliaries and Related Phenomena in a Grammar of English. *Language* 58: 591–638.

George, Alexander, ed. 1989. *Reflections on Chomsky*. Oxford: Blackwell.

Goldsmith, John. 1985. A Principled Exception to the Coordinate Structure Constraint. *Papers from the 21st Regional Meeting, Chicago Linguistic Society*, ed. by William Eilfort, Paul Kroeber, and Karen Peterson. Chicago: Chicago Linguistic Society.

Green, Georgia M. 1971. Some Implications of an Interaction among Constraints. *Papers from the Seventh Regional Meeting, Chicago Linguistic Society*, 85–100. Chicago: Chicago Linguistic Society.

Green, Georgia M. 1973a. The Derivation of a Relative Infinitive Construction. *Studies in the Linguistic Sciences* 3,1: 1–30. Urbana, IL: Department of Linguistics, University of Illinois.

Green, Georgia M. 1973b. Some Remarks on Split Controller Phenomena. *Papers from the Ninth Regional Meeting, Chicago Linguistic Society*, edited by Claudia Corum, T. Cedric Smith-Stark, and Ann Weiser, 123–138. Chicago: Chicago Linguistic Society.

Green, Georgia M. 1974. *Semantics and Syntactic Irregularity*. Bloomington: Indiana University Press.

Green, Georgia M. 1975. How to Get People to do Things with Words. Cole and Morgan, 107–142.

Green, Georgia M. 1976. Main Clause Phenomena in Subordinate Clauses. *Language* 52: 382–397.

Green, Georgia M. 1977. Do Inversions Change Grammatical Relations? *Studies in the Linguistic Sciences* 7;1: 157–181.

Green, Georgia M. 1980. Some Wherefores of English Inversion. *Language* 56: 582–602.

Green, Georgia M. 1981. Pragmatics and Syntactic Description. *Studies in the Linguistic Sciences*, 11;1: 27–37.

Green, Georgia M. 1982a. Colloquial and Literary Uses of Inversions. *Spoken and Written Language; Exploring Orality and Literacy*, ed. by D. Tannen, 119–154. Norwood, NJ: Ablex.

Green, Georgia M. 1982b. Linguistics and the Pragmatics of Language Use. *Poetics* 11: 45–76.

Green, Georgia M. 1985a. The Description of Inversions in Generalized Phrase Structure Grammar. *Proceedings of the Eleventh Annual Meeting, Berkeley Linguistics Society*, ed. by Mary Niepokuj, Mary VanClay, Vassiliki Nikiforidou and Deborah Feder, 117–145. Berkeley: University of California.

Green, Georgia M. 1985b. Subcategorization and the Account of Inversions. *Proceedings of the 1st Eastern States Conference on Linguistics*, 214–221. Columbus, OH: Ohio State University.

Green, Georgia M. 1992. Purpose Infinitives and their Relatives. *The Joy of Grammar: Festschrift for James D. McCawley*, ed. by Gary Larson, Diane Brentari, and Lynn MacLeod, 95–127. Chicago: University of Chicago Press.

Green, Georgia M. Forthcoming. Some Interactions of Pragmatics and Grammar. *Handbook of Pragmatics*, edited by Laurence R. Horn and Gregory Ward. Oxford: Blackwell.

Green, Georgia M. To appear. Elementary Principles of HPSG. *Non-transformational Syntax: A Guide to Current Models*, edited by Robert Borsley and Kersti Borjars. Oxford: Blackwell.

Green, Georgia M, and Jerry L. Morgan. 1976. Notes toward an Understanding of Rule Government. *Studies in the Linguistic Sciences* 6,1: 228–248. Urbana, IL: Department of Linguistics, University of Illinois.

Grice, H. P. 1975. Logic and Conversation. *Syntax and Semantics, Vol. 3: Speech Acts*, ed by P. Cole and J. Morgan, 43-58. New York: Academic Press.

Grinder, John. 1970. Super Equi-NP-Deletion. *Papers from the Sixth Regional Meeting, Chicago Linguistic Society*, 297–318. Chicago: Chicago Linguistic Society.

Grinder, John. 1971. A Reply to 'Super Equi-NP-Deletion as Dative Deletion.' *Papers from the Seventh Regional Meeting*, Chicago Linguistic Society, 101–11. Chicago: Chicago Linguistic Society.

Grinder, John, and Paul Postal. 1971. Missing Antecedents. *Linguistic Inquiry*: 2:269-312.

Grosu, Alexander. 1972. The Strategic Content of Island Constraints. *Ohio State University Working Papers in Linguistics* 13:1–225.

Grosu, Alexander. 1973a. On the Nonunitary Nature of the Coordinate Structure Constraint. *Linguistic Inquiry* 4:88–92.

Grosu, Alexander. 1973b. On the Status of the So-called Right-Roof Constraint. *Language* 49:294–311.

Grosu, Alexander. 1974. On the Nature of the Left Branch Constraint. *Linguistic Inquiry* 5:308–319.

Grosu, Alexander. 1975. On the Status of Positionally-Defined Constraints in Syntax. *Theoretical Linguistics* 2:159–201.

Gruber, Jeffrey. 1965. Studies in Lexical Relations. MIT dissertation. Published (1976) in Lexical Structures in Syntax and Semantics. New York: North-Holland.

Halpern, Richard. 1976. The Bivalence of NEG Raising Predicates. *Studies in the Linguistic Sciences* 6,1:69–81. Urbana, IL: Department of Linguistics, University of Illinois.

Hankamer, Jorge. 1971. Constraints on Deletion in Syntax. MIT dissertation. Abridged edition published (1977) by Garland Press, New York.

Hankamer, Jorge. 1973a. Unacceptable Ambiguity. *Linguistic Inquiry* 4:17–68.

Hankamer, Jorge. 1973b. Why There Are Two *than*'s in English. *Papers from the Ninth Regional Meeting, Chicago Linguistic Society*, edited by Claudia Corum, T. Cedric Smith-Stark, and Ann Weiser, 179–191. Chicago: Chicago Linguistic Society.

Hankamer, Jorge. 1974. On the Non-cyclic Nature of WH-clefting. *Papers from the Tenth Regional Meeting, Chicago Linguistic Society*, 221–233. Chicago: Chicago Linguistic Society,

Hankamer, Jorge. 1977. Multiple Analyses. *Mechanisms of Syntactic Change*, ed. by Charles Li, 583–607. Austin: University of Texas Press.

Hankamer, Jorge, and Ivan Sag. 1976. Deep and Surface Anaphora. *Linguistic Inquiry* 7:391–426.

Harris, Frances. 1976. Reflexivization. *Syntax and Semantics, vol. 7: Notes from the Linguistic Underground*, ed. by J. D. McCawley, 63–84. New York: Academic Press.

Harris, Richard Allen. 1993. *The Linguistics Wars*. Oxford: Oxford University Press.

Hayes, B. 1976a. Prepositional Phrase Extraposition. *Harvard Studies in Syntax and Semantics*, Vol. 2, 222–240.

Hayes, B. 1976b. The Semantic Nature of the Intervention Constraint. *Linguistic Inquiry* 7:371–375.

Hermon, Gabriella. 1979. On the Discourse Structure of Direct Quotation. Technical report 143, Center for the Study of Reading. Champaign, IL: University of Illinois.

Higgins, F. R. 1978. *The Pseudo-cleft Construction in English*. New York: Garland.

Hooper, Joan. 1973. A Critical Look at the Structure-Preserving Constraint. *Critiques of Syntactic Studies*, II, ed. by P. Schachter and G. Bedell. Los Angeles: Department of Linguistics, UCLA.

Hooper, Joan, and Sandra Thompson. 1973. On the applicability of root transformations. *Linguistic Inquiry* 4:465–497.

Horn, Laurence. 1971. Negative Transportation: Unsafe at any Speed? *Papers from the Seventh Regional Meeting, Chicago Linguistic Society*, 120–133. Chicago: Chicago Linguistic Society.

Horn, Laurence. 1975. Neg-raising Predicates: Toward an Explanation. *Papers from the Eleventh Regional Meeting, Chicago Linguistic Society*, 279–294. Chicago: Chicago Linguistic Society.

Horn, Laurence. 1979. Remarks on Neg-raising. *Syntax and Semantics, Vol. 9: Pragmatics*, ed. by P. Cole, 129–220. New York: Academic Press.

Horn, Laurence. 1986. Presupposition: Theme and Variations. *Papers from the Parasession on Pragmatics and Grammatical Theory*, 168–192. Chicago: Chicago Linguistic Society.

Horn, Laurence. 1989. *A Natural History of Negation*. Chicago: University of Chicago Press.

Huang, C.-T. James, and C.-S. Luther Liu. 2000. Logophoricity, Attitudes and *ziji* at the Interface. *Syntax and Semantics, Vol. 33: Long Distance Reflexives*, edited by Peter Cole, Gabriella Hermon, and C.-T. James Huang. San Diego, CA: Academic Press.

Jackendoff, Ray. 1972. *Semantic Interpretation in Generative Grammar*. Cambridge, MA: MIT Press.

Jackendoff, Ray. 1974. *An Introduction to the X'-Convention*. Indiana University Linguistics Club.

Jackendoff, Ray. 1977. *X'-Syntax*. Cambridge, MA: MIT Press.

Jackendoff, Ray. 1997. Lexical Insertion in a Post-Minimalist Theory of Grammar. *The Architecture of the Language Faculty*. Cambridge, MA: MIT Press.

Jacobson, Pauline. 1987. Phrase Structure, Grammatical Relations, and Discontinuous Constituents. *Syntax and Semantics, Vol. 20: Discontinuous Constituency*, ed. by Geoffrey J. Huck and Almerindo E. Ojeda, 27–70. Orlando: Academic Press.

Jacobson, Pauline, and Paul Neubauer. 1974. Extraposition Rules and the Cycle. *Berkeley Studies in Syntax and Semantics, vol. I*, ed. by Charles Fillmore, George Lakoff, and Robin Lakoff, VIII 1–99. Berkeley: University of California.

Jacobson, Pauline, and Paul Neubauer. 1976. Rule Cyclicity: Evidence from the Intervention Constraint. *Linguistic Inquiry* 7:429–461.

Jake, Janice. 1977. Gapping, Pragmatics, and Factivity. *Papers from the Thirteenth Regional Meeting, Chicago Linguistic Society*, 165–17. Chicago: Chicago Linguistic Society.

Johnson, David. 1974. On the Role of Grammatical Relations in Linguistic Theory. *Papers from the Tenth Regional Meeting, Chicago Linguistic Society*, 269–283. Chicago: Chicago Linguistic Society.

Johnson, David. 1978. *Toward a Theory of Relationally-based Grammar*. New York: Garland.

Johnson, David, and Paul Postal. 1980. *Arc-Pair Grammar*. Princeton: Princeton University Press.

Johnson, Kyle. 1991. Object Positions. *Natural Language and Linguistic Theory* 9:577–6336.

Kantor, Robert N. 1977. The Management and Comprehension of Discourse Connection by Pronouns in English. Ohio State University dissertation.

Kaplan, Ronald, and Joan Bresnan. 1982. Lexical-Functional Grammar: A Formal Theory of Grammatical Representation. *The Mental Representation of Grammatical Relations*, ed. by J. Bresnan, 173–281. Cambridge, MA: MIT Press.

Karttunen, Lauri. 1971. Definite Descriptions with Crossing Coreference; A Study of the Bach-Peters Paradox. *Foundations of Language* 7:157–182.

Katz, Jerrold J. 1981. *Language and Other Abstract Objects*. Totowa, New Jersey: Rowman and Littlefield.

Kayne, Richard. 1994. *The Antisymmetry of Syntax*. Cambridge, MA: MIT Press.

Keenan, Edward. 1975. Some Universals of Passive in Relational Grammar. *Papers from the Eleventh Regional Meeting, Chicago Linguistic Society*, 340–352. Chicago: Chicago Linguistic Society.

Keenan, Edward, and Bernard Comrie. 1977. Noun Phrase Accessibility and Universal Grammar. *Linguistic Inquiry* 8:63–99.

Kimball, John. 1971. Super Equi-NP-Deletion as Dative Deletion. *Papers from the Seventh Regional Meeting, Chicago Linguistic Society*, 142–148. Chicago: Chicago Linguistic Society.

King, Harold. 1970. On Blocking the Rules for Contraction in English. *Linguistic Inquiry* 1:134–136.

Kiparsky, Paul, and Carol Kiparsky. 1970. Fact. *Progress in Linguistics*, ed. by Manfred Bierwisch and Karl Erich Heidolph, 143–173. The Hague: Mouton. Also in *Semantics, An Interdisciplinary Reader*, ed. by Danny Steinberg and L. Jakobovits, 345–369. Cambridge University Press (1971).

Klein, Ewan, and Ivan Sag. 1982. Semantic Type and Control. *Developments in Generalized Phrase Structure Grammar*, ed. by M. Barlow, D. Flickinger, and I. Sag, 1–25. Indiana University Linguistics Club.

Koopman, Hilda. 1984. *The Syntax of Verbs*. Dordrecht: Foris.

Koutsoudas, Andreas. 1972. The Strict Order Fallacy. *Language* 48:88–96.

Koutsoudas, Andreas. 1973. Unordered Rule Hypotheses. Indiana University Linguistics Club.

Kuhn, Thomas. 1970. *The Structure of Scientific Revolutions*, 2nd ed. enlarged. International Encyclopedia of Unified Science, Vol. II, No. 2. Chicago: University of Chicago Press.

Kuno, Susumu. 1975. Three Perspectives in the Functional Approach to Syntax. *Functionalism*, ed. by R. E. Grossman, L. J. San, and T. J. Vance, 276–336. Chicago: Chicago Linguistic Society.

Kuno, Susumu, and Jane J. Robinson. 1972. Multiple WH-Questions. *Linguistic Inquiry* 3:463–487.

Ladusaw, William. 1988. A Proposed Distinction between Level and Stratum. *Linguistics in the Morning Calm*, ed. by Linguistic Society of Korea. Seoul: Hanshin Publishing Co.

Ladusaw, William and David Dowty. 1985. Towards a Non-grammatical Account of Thematic Roles. Paper presented at Santa Cruz Conference on Generative Linguistics.

Lakoff, George. 1965. On the Nature of Syntactic Irregularity. Published 1970 as *Irregularity in Syntax*. New York: Holt, Rinehart and Winston.

Lakoff, George. 1966. Deep and Surface Grammar. Dittoed ms.

Lakoff, George. 1968. Counterparts. Ms.

Lakoff, George. 1969. Pronominalization, Negation, and the Analysis of Adverbs. *Readings in English Transformational Grammar*, ed. by Roderick Jacobs and P.S. Rosenbaum, 145–165. Waltham, MA: Ginn.

Lakoff, George. 1970. Global Rules. *Language* 46:627–639.

Lakoff, George. 1971. On Generative Semantics. *Semantics, An Interdisciplinary Reader*, ed. by Danny Steinberg and L. Jakobovits, 232–296. Cambridge University Press.

Lakoff, George. 1972. Some Thoughts on Transderivational Constraints. *Papers in Linguistics in Honor of Henry and Renee Kahane*, ed. by Braj Kachru, Y. Malkiel, A. Pietrangeli, and S. Saporta, 442–452. Urbana: University of Illinois Press.

Lakoff, George. 1976. Pronouns and Reference. *Syntax and Semantics, Vol. 7: Notes from the Linguistic Underground*, ed. by J. McCawley, 276–336. New York: Academic Press. (Written in 1968)

Lakoff, George. 1986. Frame Semantic Control of the Coordinate Structure Constraint. *Papers from the 22nd Regional Meeting, Chicago Linguistic Society (Papers from the Parasession)*, ed. by Anne M. Farley, P. T. Farley, and K.-E. McCullough, 152–167. Chicago: Chicago Linguistic Society.

Lakoff, Robin. 1968. *Abstract Syntax and Latin Complementation*. Cambridge, MA: MIT Press.

Lakoff, Robin. 1969. A Syntactic Argument for *Not*-Transportation. *Papers from the Fifth Regional Meeting, Chicago Linguistic Society*, 140–148. Chicago: Chicago Linguistic Society.

Lakoff, Robin. 1971. Passive Resistance. *Papers from the Seventh Regional Meeting*, Chicago Linguistic Society, 141–162. Chicago: Chicago Linguistic Society.

Langacker, Ronald. 1966. Pronominalization and the Chain of Command. *Modern Studies in English*, ed. by David Reibel and S. Schane, 160-186. Englewood Cliffs, NJ: Prentice-Hall.

Langacker, Ronald. 1974. The Question of Q. *Foundations of Language* 11:1–39.

Lappin, Shalom. 1996. The Interpretation of Ellipsis. *Handbook of Contemporary Semantic Theory,* edited by Shalom Lappin, 145-175. Oxford: Blackwell.

Larson, Richard. 1988. On the Double Object Construction. *Linguistic Inquiry* 19:335–391

Lasnik, Howard. 1999. Pseudogapping Puzzles. Fragments: Studies in Ellipsis anad Gapping, ed. by Shalom Lappin and Abbas Benmamoun. Oxford: Oxford University Press.

Lasnik, Howard, and Mamoru Saito. 1992. *Move Alpha*. Cambridge, MA: MIT Press.

Lees, Robert. 1960. *The Grammar of English Nominalizations*. Mouton: The Hague.

Lees, Robert, and Edward Klima. 1963. Rules for English Pronominalization. *Language* 39:17–28. Reprinted (1969) in Modern Studies in English, ed. by David Reibel and S. Schane, 145–159. Englewood Cliffs, N.J.: Prentice- Hall.

Leskosky, Richard. 1973. Garbo. *Linguistic Inquiry* 4:546–549.

Levin, Nancy S. 1986. *Main Verb Ellipsis in Spoken English*. New York: Garland.

Levin, R.D. 1985. Right Node (Non-) Raising. *Linguistic Inquiry* 16:492–497.

Manzini, M. Rita. 1983. On Control and Control Theory. *Linguistic Inquiry* 14:421–446.

Marantz, Alec. 1991. Case and Licensing. *Proceedings of the Eastern States Conference on Linguistics*, 234–253. Columbus, OH: The Ohio State University.

McCawley, James D. 1968a. Concerning the Base Component of a Transformational Grammar. *Foundations of Language* 4:243–269.

McCawley, James D. 1968b. Lexical Insertion in a Transformational Grammar without Deep Structure. *Papers from the Fourth Regional Meeting, Chicago Linguistic Society*, ed. by Bill J. Darden, C.-J. N. Bailey, and A. Davison, 71–80. Chicago: Chicago Linguistic Society.

McCawley, James D. 1970. English as a VSO Language. *Language* 46:286–299.

McCawley, James D. 1971a. Tense and Time Reference in English. *Studies in Linguistic Semantics*, ed. by Charles J. Fillmore and D.T. Langendoen, 97–114. New York: Holt, Rinehart, and Winston.

McCawley, James D. 1971b. Where Do NPs Come From? *Semantics, An Interdisciplinary Reader*, ed. by Danny Steinberg and L. Jakobovits, 217–231. Cambridge University Press.

McCawley, James D. 1978a. Review of Introduction to Transformational Syntax, by A. Akmajian and F. Heny. *Studies in Language* 2:385–395.

McCawley, James D. 1978b. Relative and Relative-like Clauses. *Grammarij* 9:149–188.

McCawley, James D. 1981. The Syntax and Semantics of English Relative Clauses. *Lingua* 53: 99-149.

McCawley, James D. 1982. Parentheticals and Discontinuous Constituents. *Linguistic Inquiry* 13:91–106.

McCawley, James D. 1988. *The Syntactic Phenomena of English*. Chicago: University of Chicago Press.

Milsark, Gary. 1974. Existential Sentences in English. Ph.D. diss. MIT.

Montague, Richard. 1970. Universal Grammar. *Theoria* 36:373–398.

Montague, Richard. 1973. The Proper Theory of Quantification. *Approaches to Natural Language*, ed. by Jaakko Hintikka, J. Moravcsik, and P. Suppes. Dordrecht: Reidel.

Moortgat, Michael. 1988. *Categorial Investigations*. Dordrecht: Foris.

Morgan, Jerry L. 1968. Some Strange Aspects of *it*. *Papers from the Fourth Regional Meeting, Chicago Linguistic Society*, ed. by Bill J. Darden, C.-J. N. Bailey, and A. Davison, 81–93. Chicago: Chicago Linguistic Society.

Morgan, Jerry L. 1970. On the Criterion of Identity for Noun Phrase Deletion. *Papers from the Sixth Regional Meeting, Chicago Linguistic Society*, 380–389. Chicago: Chicago Linguistic Society.

Morgan, Jerry L. 1972a. Relative Clauses in English and Albanian. *The Chicago Which Hunt*, ed. by Paul Peranteau, J. N. Levi, and G. C. Phares, 63–72. Chicago: Chicago Linguistic Society.

Morgan, Jerry L. 1972b. Verb Agreement as a Rule of English. *Papers from the Eighth Regional Meeting, Chicago Linguistic Society*, 278–286. Chicago: Chicago Linguistic Society.

Morgan, Jerry L. 1972c. Some Problems of Verb Agreement. *Studies in the Linguistic Sciences* 2,1:84–90. Urbana: Department of Linguistics, University of Illinois.

Morgan, Jerry L. 1973. Sentence Fragments and the Notion 'Sentence'. *Issues in Linguistics; Papers in Honor of Henry and Renee Kahane*, ed. by Braj Kachru, Y. Malkiel, A. Pietrangeli, and S. Saporta, 719–751. Urbana: University of Illinois Press.

Morgan, Jerry L. 1975. Some Interactions of Syntax and Pragmatics. *Syntax and Semantics, Vol. 3: Speech Acts*, ed. by Peter Cole and J. Morgan, 289–304. New York: Academic Press.

Morgan, Jerry L. 1984. Some Problems of Agreement in English and Albanian. *Proceedings of the Tenth Annual Meeting, Berkeley Linguistics Society*. Berkeley: University of California.

Morgan, Jerry L. 1985. Some Problems of Determination in English Number Agreement. *Proceedings of the First Eastern States Conference on Linguistics*, ed. by Gloria Alvarez, Belinda Brodie, and Terry McCoy, 69–78. Columbus: Ohio State University.

Morgan, Jerry L., and Georgia M. Green. Forthcoming. Why Verb Agreement Is Not a Poster Child for Syntactic Theory. Volume in honor of James D. McCawley, ed. by Rebecca Wheeler, S. Mufwene, and E. Francis.

Nanni, Deborah. 1980. On the Surface Syntax of Constructions with *easy*-type Adjectives. *Language* 56:568–581.

Napoli, Donna Jo, and Emily Rando. 1978. Definites in *there*-sentences. *Language* 54:300–313.

Napoli, Donna Jo. 1979. *Syntactic Argumentation*. Washington, DC: Georgetown University Press.

Neubauer, Paul. 1972. Super-Equi Revisited. *Papers from the Eighth Regional Meeting, Chicago Linguistic Society*, 287–293. Chicago: Chicago Linguistic Society.

Newmeyer, Frederick. 1969. English Aspectual Verbs. *Studies in Linguistics and Language Learning*, Vol. 6. Seattle: University of Washington.

Newmeyer, Frederick. 1986. *Linguistic Theory in America*, 2nd ed. New York: Academic Press.

Ojeda, Almerindo. 1987. Discontinuity, Multidominance, and Unbounded Dependency in Generalized Phrase Structure Grammar: Some Preliminaries. *Syntax and Semantics, Vol. 20: Discontinuous Constituency*, ed. by Geoffrey J. Huck and Almerindo E. Ojeda, 257–282. Orlando: Academic Press.

Olsen, Margaret S. 1986. Some Problematic Issues in the Study of Intonation and Sentence Stress. Ph.D. dissertation. Urbana: University of Illinois.

Partee, Barbara. 1971. On the Requirement that Transformations Preserve Meaning. *Studies in Linguistic Semantics*, ed. by Charles Fillmore and D. T. Langendoen, 1-22. New York: Holt, Rinehart & Winston.

Perlmutter, David M. 1971. *Deep and Surface Structure Constraints in Syntax*. New York: Holt, Rinehart, and Winston. [revised version of 1968 MIT dissertation]

Perlmutter, David M. 1972. Evidence for Shadow Pronouns in French Relativization. *The Chicago Which Hunt*, ed. by Paul Peranteau, J. N. Levi, and G. C. Phares, 73–105. Chicago: Chicago Linguistic Society.

Perlmutter, David M. 1978. Impersonal Passives and the Unaccusative Hypothesis. *Proceedings of the Fourth Annual Meeting of the Berkeley Linguistics Society*, ed. by Jeri Jaeger, 157–189. Berkeley: University of California.

Perlmutter, David M., ed. 1983. *Studies in Relational Grammar, 1*. Chicago: University of Chicago Press.

Perlmutter, David M., and Paul M. Postal. 1977. Toward a Universal Characterization of Passivization. *Proceedings of the Third Annual Meeting, Berkeley Linguistics Society*, 394–417. Berkeley: University of California. (Reprinted in Perlmutter 1983).

Perlmutter, David M., and Paul M. Postal. 1983a. Some Proposed Laws of Basic Clause Structure. *Studies in Relational Grammar, 1*, ed. by David Perlmutter, 81–128. Chicago: University of Chicago Press.

Perlmutter, David M., and Paul M. Postal. 1983b. The Relational Succession Law. *Studies in Relational Grammar, 1*, ed. by David Perlmutter, 30–80. Chicago: University of Chicago Press.

Perlmutter, David M., and Paul M. Postal. 1984a. The 1-Advancement Exclusiveness Law. *Studies in Relational Grammar, 2*, ed. by David Perlmutter and C. Rosen, 81–125. Chicago: University of Chicago Press.

Perlmutter, David M., and Paul M. Postal. 1984b. Impersonal Passives and Some Relational Laws. *Studies in Relational Grammar, 2*, ed. by David Perlmutter and C. Rosen, 126–170. Chicago: University of Chicago Press.

Perlmutter, David M., and Carol G. Rosen. 1984. *Studies in Relational Grammar, 2*. Chicago: University of Chicago Press

Pinkham, Jessie. 1982. The Formation of Comparative Clauses in English and French. Ph.D. diss. Harvard University.

Pollard, Carl, and Ivan Sag. 1987. *Information-Based Syntax and Semantics*. Stanford, CA: Center for the Study of Language and Information.

Pollard, Carl, and Ivan Sag. 1994. *Head-Driven Phrase Structure Grammar*. Chicago: University of Chicago Press.

Pollock, Jean-Yves. 1989. Verb Movement, Universal Grammar, and the Structure of IP. *Linguistic Inquiry* 20:365–424.

Popper, Karl. 1968. *The Logic of Scientific Discovery*, 2nd ed. New York: Harper and Row.

Postal, Paul M. 1969. Underlying and Superficial Linguistic Structure. *Modern Studies in English*, ed. by David Reibel and S. Schane, 19–37. Englewood Cliffs, NJ: Prentice-Hall.

Postal, Paul M. 1970. On Coreferential Complement Subject Deletion. *Linguistic Inquiry* 1:439–500.

Postal, Paul M. 1971. *Crossover Phenomena*. New York: Holt, Rinehart, and Winston.

Postal, Paul M. 1972. On Some Rules that Are Not Successive Cyclic. *Linguistic Inquiry* 3:211–222.

Postal, Paul M. 1974. *On Raising*. Cambridge, MA: MIT Press.

Postal, Paul M. 1976. Avoiding Reference to Subject. *Linguistic Inquiry* 7:151–191.

Prince, Ellen. 1978. A Comparison of *it*-clefts and WH-clefts in Discourse. *Language* 54:883–906.

Prince, Ellen. 1981. Topicalization, Focus-Movement, and Yiddish-Movement: A Pragmatic Differentiation. *Proceedings of the Seventh Annual Meeting, Berkeley Linguistics Society*, ed. by Dan Alford, 249–264. Berkeley: University of California.

Prince, Ellen. 1984. Topicalization and Left-Dislocation: A Functional Analysis. *Discourses in Reading and Linguistics*, ed. by S. J. White and V. Teller, 213–225. *Annals of the New York Academy of Sciences*, 433. New York: New York Academy of Sciences.

Pullum, Geoffrey, 1979. *Rule Interaction and the Organization of a Grammar*. New York: Garland.

Pullum, Geoffrey. 1984. How Complex Could an Agreement System Be? *Proceedings of the First Eastern States Conference on Linguistics*, ed. by Gloria Alvarez, Belinda Brodie, and Terry McCoy, 79–103. Columbus: Ohio State University.

Pullum, Geoffrey. 1985. Assuming Some Version of X-Bar Theory. *Papers from the 21st Regional Meeting, Chicago Linguistic Society*, ed. by William Eilfort, Paul D. Kroeber, and Karen L. Peterson. Chicago: Chicago Linguistic Society.

Pullum, Geoffrey. 1989. Prospects for Generative Grammar in the 1990s. *Proceedings of the Western Conference on Linguistics, Vol. 2*, ed. by Frederick H. Brengelman, V. Samijan, and W. Wilkins, 257–276. Fresno: Department of Linguistics, California State University at Fresno.

Pullum, Geoffrey, and Deirdre Wilson. 1977. Autonomous Syntax and the Analysis of Auxiliaries. *Language* 53:741–788.

Pullum, Geoffrey, and Arnold Zwicky. 1984. The Syntax-Phonology Boundary and Current Syntactic Theories. *Ohio State University Working Papers in Linguistics* 29:105–116. Columbus, Ohio: Department of Linguistics, Ohio State University.

Pyle, Charles. 1972. How to Cycle without One. *Internal Journal of Linguistics*. Ann Arbor, MI: Department of Linguistics, University of Michigan.

Quirk, Randolph, Sidney Greenbaum, Geoffrey Leech, and Jan Svartvik. 1972. *A Grammar of Contemporary English*. New York: Seminar Press

Reibel, David. and Sanford Schane. 1969. *Modern Studies in English*. Englewood Cliffs, NJ: Prentice-Hall.

Reinhart, Tanya. 1983. *Anaphora and Semantic Interpretation*. Chicago: University of Chicago Press.

Reinhart, Tanya, and Eric Reuland. 1993. Reflexivity. *Linguistic Inquiry* 24:657–720.

Rizzi, Luigi. 1990. *Relativized Minimality*. Cambridge, MA: MIT Press.

Rosenbaum, Peter S. 1967. *The Grammar of English Predicate Complement Constructions*. Cambridge, MA: MIT Press.

Ross, John R. 1967. Constraints on Variables in Syntax. MIT dissertation. (Published 1983 as *Infinite Syntax*. Norwood, NJ: Ablex).

Ross, John R. 1969a. Guess Who. *Papers from the Fifth Regional Meeting, Chicago Linguistic Society*, 252–287. Chicago: Chicago Linguistic Society.

Ross, John R. 1969b. The Cyclic Nature of English Pronominalization. Reprinted in *Modern Studies in English*, ed. by David Reibel and S. Schane, 187–200. Englewood Cliffs, N.J.: Prentice-Hall. Originally published (1967) in *To Honor Roman Jakobson, II*, 1669-1682. The Hague: Mouton.

Ross, John R. 1969c. Adjectives as Noun Phrases. *Modern studies in English*, ed. by David Reibel and S. Schane, 352-360. Englewood Cliffs, NJ: Prentice-Hall.

Ross, John R. 1970a. Gapping and the Order of Constituents. *Progress in Linguistics*, ed. by Manfred Bierwisch and K. Heidolph, 249–259. The Hague: Mouton.

Ross, John R. 1970b. On Declarative Sentences. *Readings in English Transformational Grammar*, ed. by Roderick A. Jacobs and P. S. Rosenbaum, 222–272. Waltham, MA: Ginn.

Ross, John R. 1972a. Act. *Semantics of Natural Languages*, ed. by Gilbert Harman and D. Davidson, 70–126. Dordrecht: Reidel.

Ross, John R. 1972b. Doubl-*ing*. *Linguistic Inquiry* 3:61–86.

Ross, John R. 1973. Slifting. *The Formal Analysis of Natural Language*, ed. by Maurice Gross et al., 133–169. The Hague: Mouton.

Sadock, Jerrold. 1969. Hypersentences. *Papers in Linguistics* 1:283–371.

Sadock, Jerrold M. 1983. The necessary overlapping of grammatical components. *Papers from the parasession on the interplay of phonology, morphology, and syntax*, ed. by John F. Richardson, M. Marks, and A. Chukerman, 198–221. Chicago: Chicago Linguistic Society.

Sadock, Jerrold. 1987. Discontinuity in Autolexical and Autosemantic Syntax. *Syntax and Semantics, Vol. 20: Discontinuous Constituency*, ed. by Geoffrey J. Huck and Almerindo E. Ojeda, 283–303. Orlando: Academic Press.

Sag, Ivan. 1977. Deletion and Logical Form. MIT dissertation. Distributed by Indiana University Linguistics Club.

Sag, Ivan. 1979. The Non-unity of Anaphora. *Linguistic Inquiry* 10:152–164.

Sag, Ivan. 1997. English Relative Clause Constructions. *Journal of Linguistics* 33:431–483.

Sag, Ivan, Gerald Gazdar, Thomas Wasow, and Steven Weisler. 1985. Coordination and How to Distinguish Categories. *Natural Language and Linguistic Theory* 3:117–172.

Sag, Ivan and Ewan Klein. 1982. The Syntax and Semantics of English Expletive Pronoun Constructions. *Developments in Generalized Phrase Structure Grammar*, ed. by M. Barlow, D. Flickinger, and I. Sag, 92–136.

Sag, Ivan and Thomas Wasow. 1999. *Syntactic Theory: A Formal Introduction*. Stanford: CA: CSLI Publications.

Schmerling, Susan. 1973. Subjectless Sentences and the Notion of Surface Structure. *Papers from the Ninth Regional Meeting, Chicago Linguistic Society*, edited by Claudia Corum, T. Cedric Smith-Stark, and Ann Weiser, 577–586. Chicago: Chicago Linguistic Society.

Schmerling, Susan. 1978. Synonymy Judgements as Syntactic Evidence. *Syntax and Semantics, Vol. 9: Pragmatics*, edited by Peter Cole, 299–313. New York: Academic Press.

Sells, Peter. 1985. *Lectures on Contemporary Syntactic Theories*. Stanford, Calif.: Center for the Study of Language and Information.

Sheintuch, Gloria. 1975. Subject-Raising: A Unitary Rule? *Studies in the Linguistic Sciences* 5;1:125–153. Urbana: Department of Linguistics, University of Illinois.

Siegel, Dorothy. 1973. Non-sources of Unpassives. *Syntax and Semantics, Vol. 2*, ed. by John Kimball, 301–317. New York: Academic Press.

Smith, Lawrence R., and Gail G. Johnsen. 1981. *A Bibliovect Guide to the Literature in English and Theoretical Syntax*. St. John's: Information Reduction Research.

Sportiche, Dominique. 1988. A Theory of Floating Quantifiers and its Corollaries for Constituent Structure. *Linguistic Inquiry* 19:425–449.

Steever, Sandy. 1977. Raising, Meaning, and Conversational Implicature. *Papers from the Ninth Regional Meeting, Chicago Linguistic Society*, edited by Claudia Corum, T. Cedric Smith-Stark, and Ann Weiser, 590–602. Chicago: Chicago Linguistic Society.

Stockwell, Robert, Paul Schachter, and Barbara Partee. 1973. *The Major Syntactic Structures of English*. New York: Holt, Rinehart, and Winston.

Stowell, Tim. 1981. Origins of Phrase Structure. Ph.D. dissertation, Massachusetts Institute of Technology.

Stucky, Susan. 1987. Configurational Variation in English: A Study of Extraposition and Related Matters. *Syntax and Semantics, Vol. 20: Discontinuous Constituency*, ed. by Geoffrey J. Huck and Almerindo E. Ojeda, 377–405. Orlando: Academic Press.

Ward, Gregory. 1983. A Pragmatic Analysis of Epitomization: Topicalization It's Not. *Papers in Linguistics* 17:145-161.

Ward, Gregory. 1985. *The Semantics and Pragmatics of Preposing*. Ph. D. diss., University of Pennsylvania. (Published 1988 in Outstanding Dissertations in Linguistics series. New York: Garland)

Ward, Gregory. 1990. The Discourse Functions of VP Preposing. *Language* 66:742-763.

Williams, Timothy. 1995. A Pragmatic Accoount of Control. Ph.D. diss., University of Illinois.

Ziv, Yael. 1975. On the Relevance of Content to the Form-Function Correlation. *Functionalism*, ed. by R. E. Grossman, L. J. San, and T. J. Vance, 568–579. Chicago: Chicago Linguistic Society.

Ziv, Yael. 1976. Functions of Relative Clauses in English and Hebrew. Ph.D. dissertation, University of Illinois.

Zribi-Hertz, Anne. 1989. Anaphor Binding and Narrative Point of View. *Language* 65:695-727.

Zwicky, Arnold. 1973. The Analytic Leap: From 'Some Xs are Ys' to 'All Xs Are Ys.' *Papers from the Ninth Regional Meeting, Chicago Linguistic Society*, edited by Claudia Corum, T. Cedric Smith-Stark, and Ann Weiser, 700–709. Chicago: Chicago Linguistic Society.

INDEX

Subject Index